"I am alive today because of the kind of bold praying you'll find in *Pray Big*. This important book can change your expectations about prayer, challenging you to seek God much more intimately, to ask for audacious requests more boldly, and to see big answers to prayer that change lives for eternity. I highly recommend it!"

Don Piper, bestselling author, *90 Minutes in Heaven*

"Will Davis Jr. does two important things well: he challenges you to rethink some of the ideas you have ceased to think about because they are such a central part of your life, and he writes in such a graceful and natural style that you feel as though you are conversing with him. Although I have never had the opportunity to have a real conversation with him, I feel as though I have known him well for a long time."

Dr. **John M. Lilley**, president, Baylor University

"Will Davis has furnished his readers with a wonderful perspective on the relationship and communication between God and man. *Pray Big* has challenged my thinking, made sense of my struggle with prayer, and reminded me of God's power and promises."

Cody Carlson, businessman and former NFL quarterback

"Will Davis is onto something powerful. His honest and straightforward style has opened my eyes to untapped spiritual resources. This book has literally changed the way I pray!"

Dr. **Samuel Adams**, coauthor, *Out of Control*

"Effective prayer—we all want it! Will Davis's writing is intriguing as a practical, focused, and Scripture-based reference tool to enhance a believer's prayer life. Essential for both the young believer and the mature Christian, this book causes the life of prayer to come alive. A must-read for all."

Alan T. Nagel, director, City Resource Team, Europe and Russia; Campus Crusade for Christ

"Words of wisdom from a young man I've known since his college days over twenty years ago. He walks and talks the Word of God now just as he did then. No one person I have ever met believes more strongly in prayer than Will.

"A powerful book for Christians and seekers alike. Chapter 5 alone makes this a must-read book. It will change your life!"

Bob Hughes, chairman, Prime II Investments

"When Will asked me to read and provide an endorsement for his book about prayer, I was happy to do so, but I expected it to be along the lines of 'pray without ceasing' and 'pray for the lost.' The book was nothing like what I expected; instead it rocked my spiritual life, causing me to pray very differently. It inspired me to discuss everything with God, from my simplest concerns to those things that seem impossible if not for faith in God. It's grounded in Scripture with practical, realistic, and simple explanations of why we should pray, what we should pray about (everything), and how we should pray (simply and pointedly). I love Will's exhortation to pray big, hairy, audacious prayers (BHAPs). It is my hope that Christians everywhere will read this book, and that the changes God would make in our world with Christians praying BHAPs would be incalculable!"

Marcia K. Byrd, attorney-at-law

"Thanks, Will! I've got my BHAPs; I've got my pinpoint prayers; I've got a more regular prayer time, place, and plan. As a result, I'm praying more, I'm praying simpler, and I'm seeing my prayers answered! Your book has been a real encouragement to me about how God longs for us to talk with him and how he is waiting to respond. It has reenergized my spiritual life. Thank you for your insights."

Dr. **Andy W. Neillie**, president,
Deep in the Heart Leadership Group

"Simple, unparalleled prayer advice for every situation—in the everyday or in a crisis, for individuals or for groups. The book addresses to-the-point prayers and gives great biblical examples as well as Will's personal examples of prayers being answered. No situation is too small for God's attention, and this type of praying increases our communication and dependence on God. This can only be good for us. Many of us tend to pray in generalizations, afraid we will offend God by asking for the wrong thing. This book has certainly impacted my prayer life, and I feel much closer to God on a daily basis (although he may get tired of me asking for help in finding lost keys).

"After I read this book, I started praying pinpoint prayers. I've used the book's themes every day and in a recent crisis situation. They have been very comforting and helpful.

"Very inspirational. Prayer is a vital part of personal happiness in anyone's life."

Drue Dillard Corbusier, executive vice president,
Dillard's Department Stores

PRAY BIG

the power of pinpoint prayers

WILL DAVIS JR.

Revell

a division of Baker Publishing Group
Grand Rapids, Michigan

Published by Revell
a division of Baker Publishing Group
P.O. Box 6287, Grand Rapids, MI 49516-6287
www.revellbooks.com

Third printing, April 2008

Printed in the United States of America

Library of Congress Cataloging-in-Publication Data
Davis, Will, 1962–
    Pray big : the power of pinpoint prayers / Will Davis, Jr.
      . p.   cm.
    Includes bibliographical references.
    ISBN 10: 0-8007-3204-9 (pbk.)
    ISBN 978-0-8007-3204-2 (pbk.)
    1. Prayer—Christianity. I. Title.
BV210.3.D38 2007
248.3′2—dc22   2006037330

Dedicated to the memory of "Little Management,"
Carie Lynn Fontenot—fellow Christ-follower,
ACF staff member, and good friend

Thanks to the following people:

- Susie, Will III, Emily, and Sara—for being the greatest family ever and for loving me unconditionally
- Rick Reynolds—for keeping me in the game
- Les Stobbe—for taking a risk on me
- Bill Jensen—for first believing in me and encouraging me to keep writing
- Wendy Browning—for tireless and selfless service. You are amazing!
- Teri Crow—for being able to provide awesome proofreading services and have a baby at the same time!
- The Austin Christian Fellowship family—for being a praying church and for putting up with me
- The ACF overseers—for giving me permission to write
- The ACF staff—for giving me grace when I'm out writing
- Joni Kendrick—for being a great friend and for listening to me rant on and on about this book
- Julie Crain Washington—for being a great staff translator
- Stephanie Morton—for including me in her search process and for allowing me to tell her story
- Wendy and Jim Jimmerson—for sharing Abby's story and for being such godly examples
- Ralph Smith—for being my pastor
- Isabel Nelson—for modeling simple, childlike prayer
- David Walker—for praying that I would love to pray

Contents

1

LORD, TEACH US TO PRAY
Pinpoint Praying for Beginners

This, then, is how you should pray.
Matthew 6:9

I believe in prayer.
I believe in prayer totally, absolutely. I know it works. I became a "believer" after about the five hundredth coincidence between events and my prayers. After a while, you start to get the feeling that something's up.

Let me give you an example. Recently I flew from my home in Austin, Texas, to Chicago to interview three potential staff members for our church. My 6:15 a.m. flight to O'Hare was delayed by weather and by the crew's need for adequate rest. When I finally got to O'Hare, I sat from 9:30 a.m. to 3:30 p.m. in the same booth of an airport restaurant while I met with the three candidates. (I think my waitress thought I was part of some CIA conspiratorial meeting. She probably never quite figured out why I was having a series of strange meetings with different people.) After my last appointment, I walked back to the gate, exhausted, only to face more weather delays, noisy crowds, and cramped quarters.

Once I finally snuggled into seat 22B on my flight back to Austin, I did my best to avoid any real conversation with the guy in 22A. He quickly ordered three beers and seemed content to sit and sip while I sat and sulked. I was tired and irritable and wanted to be left alone. Things were on their way to a conversation-free two-hour flight when suddenly the guy in 22A started talking. It seemed the Michelob Light had loosened his tongue.

The man's name was Scott. He was thirty-two, recently divorced, and on his way to Fort Hood, Texas, for deployment to the Middle East. It didn't take long for me to discern that Scott was probably not a believer and that he was lonely and hurting.

Serious bummer. I am a pastor and, more importantly, a Christian. I'm the perfect candidate to help a guy like Scott. But (I'm ashamed to admit) I didn't want to. My emotional tanks were near empty, and I was ready to be "off duty" for the rest of that already long day. Knowing that God expects me to be alert to such opportunities and to steward them well, however, I prayed, *Father, I'm really tired, and I could use some rest. But if you want me to talk to this guy, then please show me.*

I hadn't even finished praying those last two words when Scott turned to me and said, "So, what do you do for a living?" Great. I actually laughed and shook my head at God's sense of humor before I turned to Scott and said, "I'm a pastor." Now, telling someone you're a pastor can kill a conversation. But not this one. Scott looked like he had just won the lottery. For the next two hours, we talked about his divorce, his childhood, the death of his stepfather, his cousin's recent alcohol-related car wreck that killed an innocent young girl, his upcoming deployment, death and heaven, the resurrection of Jesus, and the veracity of the Gospels. Before we were done, the man in the seat in front of Scott had joined in the conversation. He was a district judge from Louisiana who had just completed a two-week mission trip in India helping the survivors of the 2004 tsunami. I was fully expecting "Amazing Grace" to play through the plane's PA system at any moment.

Like I said, I believe in prayer.

Do you? If so, then what follows will inspire you, encourage you, and quite possibly forever change the way you approach prayer and what you expect from it. Are you ready to have a huge burst of spiritual adrenaline added to your prayer life?

Fat-Free Praying

"Can we talk about prayer?" That's basically the question the disciples asked Jesus on more than one occasion in the Gospels. Jesus's disciples certainly weren't prayer rookies. They knew temple prayers, synagogue prayers, and all the festival prayers. They knew the prayers of David, the intercessions of Samuel, and the laments of Jeremiah. But when Jesus prayed, they heard and saw an altogether different level of prayer, and it made them thirsty for more.

"Can we talk about prayer?" Or, stated more literally, "Lord, teach us to pray." Even though these men were not prayer lightweights, their exposure to Jesus showed them they still had much to learn. On one occasion when the disciples asked Jesus about prayer, he responded by teaching them the most recited prayer in history.

> This, then, is how you should pray:
> "Our Father in heaven,
> hallowed be your name,
> your kingdom come,
> your will be done
>   on earth as it is in heaven.

Give us today our daily bread.
Forgive us our debts,
    as we also have forgiven our debtors.
And lead us not into temptation,
but deliver us from the evil one."

Matthew 6:9–13

You know those words and have probably prayed them on countless occasions. But have you ever noticed the pure simplicity of this prayer? Have you noted its brevity and clarity? Jesus obviously was giving us a model outline for how our prayers might flow. But as a simple prayer, the Lord's Prayer is the perfect example of what I call *pinpoint praying*. There's no fluff, no fat, no extra words or theologically heavy terms. There's just simple, spot-on, pinpoint accuracy from Jesus. With a mere fifty-eight Greek words, Jesus acknowledged the character and sovereignty of God, surrendered to the Father's will, and sought provision, protection, and guidance from God. That's pinpoint praying.

"Lord, Please Be with Tom and Jill. Please Bless Joe and Sally and Be with Sue. . . ."

Have you ever walked away from a prayer session wondering what, if anything, you actually accomplished? I certainly have. I was thinking about that recently after spending the better part of a morning in prayer with a group of other believers. It was a sweet time. We shared much love with both the Lord and each other. We offered praises, confessions, and thanksgivings. We prayed for the sick, the brokenhearted, and the lost. We prayed for provision and direction. But as I walked away from that meeting, I couldn't shake the gnawing feeling that we hadn't accomplished all that we could have.

> We need to pray for things—very specific things, gritty things, personal things, important things, kingdom things—with the pinpoint precision that Jesus modeled in the Lord's Prayer.

Have you ever listened to how we pray? It's like Christians have developed their own prayer language, and I don't mean the ecstatic kind. *Lord, please bless Bill.* What exactly do we mean by that? Do we want God to make Bill more holy or more disciplined? Are we hoping that his business will prosper or that he'll be a better husband? And why do we ask for blessing when Ephesians 1:3 says that we are already blessed with every spiritual blessing that God can give? *God, please be with Joan.* God's already with Joan. His Spirit lives in her, and he promised to never leave or forsake her. What do we really want God to do for Joan? *Father, we pray that you give Jack a special anointing.* As if there is such a thing as an ordinary anointing. *Special anointing* is redundant. *And, God, we ask that you give Sue an extra helping of your grace.* What is that? Does God dole out grace in measured proportions? That prayer makes God seem as if he has a big serving spoon—that he can be either generous or stingy with the helpings of grace he dispenses.

God wants us to be strategic and focused about what we're asking him to do. We need to pray for things—very specific things, gritty things, personal things, important things, kingdom things—with the pinpoint precision that Jesus modeled in the Lord's Prayer.

What do you really need? What walls need tearing down, and what strongholds need obliterating? What captives need freeing, and what lost people need saving? What Christian-led businesses in your city do you want to prosper, and what strip joints and adult bookstores do you want

to see shut down? What termi-
nally ill person do you want to
see healed? What poor or un-
ethical leaders need to either

At its core, pinpoint
praying is simple.

change their ways or be removed from leadership, and
what godly leaders need to be given more of a platform?
What do you really want and need God to do? Whatever it
is, if you're serious about receiving it from God, then you
need to pray with the same focus that Jesus did.

When You Pray, Keep It Simple!

The great news is that pinpoint praying doesn't require
a master's degree in principles of advanced theological
and spiritual dialogue. In fact, it's just the opposite. If
anything, pinpoint praying is what you're most likely to
do when left to yourself. It's the childlike, straightforward
kind of communication with God that Jesus applauded
in the Gospels and modeled in his own ministry. At its
core, pinpoint praying is simple.

We've made prayer too complicated. My own book-
shelves and hard drives are filled with guides, tools, and
aids that are supposed to help me pray better. The problem is that I have to learn the program or concepts on
which each of these well-meaning tools is based. I can
actually spend more time learning the program and setting up the notebook, journal, flash cards, or software
than I do praying. For me, these "aids" often complicate
rather than simplify the process.

I remember my first venture into the complicated
world of voice recognition software. For just $249.99,
I was going to be freed from ever handwriting or typ-
ing another letter or note again. Gone for me were the
dark ages of pen, paper, and keyboards. Now I would
be able to just talk to my computer, and it would print

everything I said. There was only one small catch: I had to learn to speak the computer's language. In order for my computer to understand what I was saying, I had to speak its new techno jargon. With the voice-recognition software came a book of rules I had to follow and expressions I had to use if my computer and I were going to talk to each other. The user-friendly guide promised success after just a few tries. Right.

I've had over thirty-five hours of college and master's level Greek, six hours of master's level Hebrew, and six hours of advanced theological German, so you would think that learning to speak "computer" would have been easy for me. Not a chance. Learning ancient Greek and Hebrew was a breeze compared to learning to speak to a computer! I was lost before I ever started. The only communication that happened between me and my computer was when I spoke at it, not with it, and typically I wasn't saying very nice things.

We've made prayer just as difficult. Somehow we've gotten the impression that true prayer requires big words, lengthy phrases, and choice theological terms. But that's not what Jesus modeled for us. He taught his prayer-hungry disciples to pray with focus, confidence, specificity, and brevity. What a concept! If you want to be razor-sharp in your praying, tell God what you're thinking in the most direct, blunt, and simple terms possible. Pray in a language that you understand, and then trust that God will get it.

The Makings of a Pinpoint Prayer

There are two basic principles in effective pinpoint praying, and both are easy for you to master. The first is *be specific*. Reread the Lord's Prayer and see if you can find any vague or nonspecific wording. Everything Jesus spoke had focus and clarity. It's as if he aimed the bow and arrows of intercession at the bull's-eye of what he wanted and needed from God, and then he started shooting. Think about what Jesus shot at in the Lord's Prayer.

> **Target**: God's glory. **Pinpoint Prayer**: *Let your name be honored and exalted.*
>
> **Target**: God's agenda. **Pinpoint Prayer**: *Let your kingdom and will function in my life today with the same efficiency and ease as they do in heaven.*
>
> **Target**: God's provision. **Pinpoint Prayer**: *Please give me today everything that I need.*
>
> **Target**: Relational health. **Pinpoint Prayer**: *Please forgive me and help me to be forgiving.*
>
> **Target**: God's protection. **Pinpoint Prayer**: *Keep me free from temptation and rescue me when I am assaulted by evil.*

Do you see the precision and purpose with which Jesus approached God? There was nothing fuzzy or hazy about what he was seeking. Jesus understood that prayer was the most important spiritual activity a human could engage in, and he practiced it with refreshing single-mindedness and simplicity.

Are your prayers specific? When you approach God, do you know what you're aiming at? Do you show the same precision and force that Jesus did? A high volume of words isn't required to get through to God in prayer. Lofty, poetically painted pictures don't necessarily hit the target you're aiming for. Specific, forceful, pinpoint precision does. Tell God what you need in the simplest, most childlike terms possible.

The second principle of pinpoint praying is *be biblical*. Use the Bible to help formulate the wording of your prayers. Isaiah promised us that no word that comes from God's mouth will ever fail in its divine purpose (see Isa. 55:11). The writer of Hebrews added that God's Word is living, active, and sharper than any double-edged sword (see Heb. 4:12). So it makes sense to pray as much of the Bible back to God as you can. It's the best prayer script ever written.

Praying the Bible takes all the guesswork out of prayer. Right at your fingertips there is an arsenal of pinpoint prayers that you know God will answer. Why spend time trying to figure out how to word your requests and needs to God when the Bible has already done it for you? Instead of struggling with what to say, just pray God's holy Word right back to him.

Before we go any farther, please go get your Bible. Now look at that awesome resource you have in your hands. Do you want to blow the roof off your prayers? Do you want to see impact, life transformation, and blessing that you never thought possible? Do you want to receive God-sized, kingdom-level answers to your prayers? Then pull your prayers from the pages of God's incredible, inspired, and anointed prayer book. Commit right now to make your Bible the center of your prayer life.

Isabel's Prayer

I first met Isabel at our church's membership class. She attended with her husband and stayed after to ask me some pointed questions about her faith. Isabel had some serious emotional and relational baggage that was keeping her from experiencing God's love. She had built a massive wall around her heart, and it was obvious that the Holy Spirit had his work cut out for him. Isabel's heart would not be an easy one to reach.

Several weeks later, I met with Isabel in my office for a follow-up visit. She had made tremendous progress. The distance between her and God had closed dramatically. The more we talked, the more I sensed that Isabel was ready to yield her heart completely to Christ. Her questions, although not completely gone, had basically been answered. She could see no reason to keep her heart back from Jesus any longer. I told Isabel to just start talking to Jesus and to tell him what she wanted and needed him to do. I don't know what I expected to happen, but I certainly wasn't prepared for what she did.

Isabel slipped out of her chair and dropped to her knees right in front of me. She interlocked her fingers and then placed them just below her chin. In that humble position, with her head bowed and her eyes closed, Isabel looked like a beautiful seven-year-old. She prayed like one too.

Isabel told God that she wanted to be a Christian. She asked him to forgive her sins, to remove her doubts and fears, to heal her wounds, and to be her Savior. She told God that she was completely surrendering her life to Jesus as best she could. Isabel's prayer was one of the sweetest, most tender prayers I've ever heard. When she got up off her knees, we both knew she had been changed.

Isabel's problems didn't go away that day. She continued to struggle with the emotional and relational pain that had originally distanced her from God. But Isabel had something she didn't have previously—the Holy Spirit. She knew she was a Christian. She still had her battles to fight, but she was no longer fighting them alone.

Did you notice the two ingredients of pinpoint praying in Isabel's words? First, she was specific. This was no *Lord, please bless and be with me* prayer. Isabel went right into the presence of God with her specific needs: *Lord, please forgive me*; *Lord, please save me*; *Lord, please accept my unconditional surrender*; *Lord, please heal me.*

With those simple petitions, Isabel launched pinpoint intercessory missiles straight into the heart of heaven. She left no room for doubt in her heart of what she was asking God to do. She prayed with pinpoint accuracy.

She was also biblical. There is no more biblical prayer than that of a sinner seeking restoration to God. From Genesis 1 to Revelation 22, the Bible shows that God is ready to save and forgive any person who will seek him. The purpose of God's entire redemptive plan is to bring us back to him. When a sinner breathes out a humble petition for salvation, he or she doesn't have to wonder if God will answer. His answer has already been fully displayed in the cross of Jesus.

When Isabel went to her knees in my office and began to plead her case before God, she couldn't have been on more biblical ground. The road into God's holy presence had already been paved for her by Jesus's holy blood. The answer to her prayer had already been uttered by Jesus when he declared, "It is finished!" on the cross. The assurance that Jesus was powerful enough to save Isabel was demonstrated when he rose from the dead. And the promise that Jesus would save Isabel was delivered when he sent his Holy Spirit into the world to woo every last sinner to himself. When Isabel sought God's salvation in prayer, she spoke the most moving, anointed, holy, eternal, and effective pinpoint prayer a person can give. And God's answer, before she even finished her first word, was yes!

Isabel's prayer for salvation is the first of countless pinpoint prayers that God promises to answer. There's never been a sinner seeking God's forgiveness who was sent away unforgiven or told to come back later. Isn't that amazing? You can fall to your knees right now, humbly and genuinely seeking God's mercy and forgiveness, and know that he will answer you. Do you need to have a moment like Isabel did? Don't wait any longer.

Put down this book, get on your knees, and tell God in specific language that you need his forgiveness and that you are surrendering to Jesus. That's a pinpoint prayer that God always answers.

Faith Made Easy

If you're a Christian, you need to know that you have already asked God for the greatest miracle that he can grant a person—and his answer was yes. Without question, the greatest miracle you can ever seek from God is the saving of a lost soul. When God brings salvation to a person, he cancels the curse of sin, reverses the effects of death, frees a captive from Satan, and secures the person forever in his heavenly kingdom. That's the biggest miracle that God can ever perform. It requires more power and more sacrifice than anything else you can ask God to do. Why? Because it required the death of his Son.

God parted the Red Sea, sent multiple plagues upon the Egyptians, opened blind eyes, caused the mute to speak, straightened crooked limbs, cast out demons, and even raised the dead, all without having to kill his own Son. But when it came to setting sinners free, the death and resurrection of Jesus was required. Nothing was ever more demanding for our holy God. Creation—the forming of the universe, the earth, and the laws that govern them—was easy for God compared to what it cost him to save you and me.

When sinners pray to a holy God and ask for salvation, they're asking God to once again reverse the natural course of the laws of sin and death. They're asking God to waive justice and to grant mercy. They're asking God to do something far beyond what any human could ever do, something far greater than any other miracle in the

Bible. And God's answer every single time is yes. The Bible supports this with dozens of promises. Jesus put it this way: "Whoever comes to me I will never drive away" (John 6:37).

If God's answer to the most demanding pinpoint prayer is always yes; if God has never said no to that which requires the highest output of his love, power, and grace; and if the pinpoint prayer of a lost sinner can so move God, then how do you think he'll respond when his children ask him for other things that are specific and biblical? When you're pinpoint praying for financial provision, for revival to come to a town, for prodigals to return home, for the sick to be healed, for marriages to be saved, for the godly to be promoted, or for children to be protected, you're asking God to do what he said he would—and something much easier than saving a lost soul. When you pray biblically and specifically, when you have the scope of your prayer aimed right at the heart of God, when you're asking God for what he said he can and will do, know that you're on solid ground with God. Don't be timid or shy; ask boldly and confidently. God has already promised that he will come through.

What Lies Ahead

In the coming chapters, we will look at pinpoint prayers for our common, everyday situations. We'll learn about miracle praying, and we'll see why praying for seemingly mundane and unimportant things is actually very important. We'll learn how to pray for the spiritually lost and how to pray when we're walking through a crisis. We'll discover the importance of praying with other Christians and why group prayer is the most powerful form of pinpoint praying. We'll see how to pray for spouses, for children, and even for ourselves. Finally, we'll learn how to pray when we're so wounded spiritually that we don't think we can. In every case, we'll apply the simple principles of pinpoint prayer.

God gave us the tool of prayer for a reason. He loaded his Word with promises that inspire us to pray. He's already shown us that he's willing to grant the most difficult and demanding request we can ever make of him. Let's learn to use specific and biblical pinpoint prayers as God intended. God is waiting to release all the power of heaven itself to those who will ask him.

Discussion Questions

1. When was the last time you had an obvious answer to one of your prayers? What happened?
2. Why do you think we resort to or settle for the *Lord, be with Bill* and *Lord, bless Sue* types of prayers? Why don't we typically pray with more focus or effort?
3. Think about your typical prayers. How specific and biblical are they? What types of things are you asking God for right now? Do they meet the criteria of pinpoint prayers?
4. How might the content of your prayers be changed to be more focused and effective?
5. If you are a Christian, you now know that God has already granted the greatest request you can make of him—salvation. How has that knowledge affected your faith? How might it affect the way you pray?
6. After reading this chapter, what is one change you intend to make in the way you pray?

2

BIG, HAIRY, AUDACIOUS PRAYERS
Pinpoint Praying for Miracles

Do not be afraid, Zechariah; your prayer has been heard.
Your wife Elizabeth will bear you a son.

Luke 1:13

Here are some dangerous questions: What are you praying for today that will require a miraculous answer from God? What are you asking for that only God can do? If you seem to be stuck in a prayer rut, if your "asks" are limited to the token *God, bless Joe* and *God, be with Sherri* kinds of requests, then it's time for you to start taking some risks in prayer. It's time for you to start asking big.

Let me offer you an example. Two thousand years ago, an elderly man moved silently about his priestly work in the inner chambers of the temple. His name was Zechariah, and he was chosen by lot to perform the priestly duty of interceding for the nation and offering incense and prayers to God. It was a high honor. Many priests would live their entire lives and never be

23

chosen for such a task. Zechariah would get to perform this priestly function only once in his life. While he was inside offering prayers for the nation, a crowd gathered outside the inner courts and was praying for him. They were interceding for the intercessor. Now, there's a concept.

As Zechariah moved about inside the temple, the inner court was suddenly flooded with white light, and Zechariah realized that he was in the presence of an angel. Needless to say, he was terrified. It seemed that the angelic messenger brought unlikely news: "Do not be afraid, Zechariah; your prayer has been heard. Your wife Elizabeth will bear you a son, and you are to give him the name John" (Luke 1:13).

Now, that news may not seem like such a big deal, certainly not one meriting angelic announcement. Couples find out every day that they're expecting without any fanfare whatsoever. But this was obviously no ordinary pregnancy. Scripture tells us that Zechariah and his wife, Elizabeth, were well beyond their childbearing years. Besides that, Elizabeth's womb was barren. She had never been able to bear children. For a woman in first-century Palestine, few fates could be worse. Much shame and scorn fell upon a woman who could not preserve her husband's name through childbirth. Elizabeth and Zechariah were facing the end of their lives without having the ability to do anything about their childlessness.

But did you catch what the angel said? Just before he announced that they were to be proud parents, he said, "Your prayer has been heard." What prayer? Had Zechariah and Elizabeth been praying for a child? Had they been patiently asking God to end Elizabeth's barrenness and to give them a baby? Apparently so, because the angel declared that their son would be born as a direct result of their requests to God.

Knowing that fact about Zechariah and Elizabeth makes me like and respect them even more. Can you imagine anything bolder, anything more daring than asking God to give an elderly couple a son? These two "believers" had the spiritual gumption to believe that not only *could* God open a closed womb but he *would* do it. They weren't *God, be with Tom* and *God, bless Joe* pray-ers. They knew what they wanted, and even though it was humanly impossible, they had the audacity to ask God for it.

You have to admire their faith. Certainly they had heard the accounts of God granting Abraham and Sarah a son in their later years. Zechariah and Elizabeth knew that God had done such a thing before, and they were just courageous enough to ask him to do it again. They were asking God to do something that they could not, something only he could, and something that would no doubt be registered in the "miracle" department.

Think about your prayers. What are you asking of God that only he can do? Are you seeking that which could be registered only in the "miracle" department when it happens? If you were *really* sure that God hears and answers your prayers, would it change the way you pray? In short, are you asking big? Do you believe that we *should* ask big things of God? Is he pleased or put off when we seek the miraculous from him?

The Bible teaches that such praying is neither arrogant nor irresponsible. In fact, both Testaments of the Bible endorse the principle of praying big. It's the kind of praying that the Old Testament leaders and heroes engaged in. It's the kind of praying that Jesus both modeled and encouraged. And it's the kind of praying that we need to practice.

Do you make big asks of God? Don't be timid in your prayers. Prayer should be as big as God's promises and as full as God's resources. Your requests should require the full power and provision of God.

Asking Big

In his bestselling book *Built to Last*, management and leadership expert Jim Collins examined profitable companies whose years of success lasted well beyond the founding leader's tenure. He wanted to know what characterized companies that survived and even thrived after transitioning from their original leader to a second- or third-generation leader. Collins listed several key attributes of such great companies, but one characteristic stood out from all the rest and became the trademark message of Collins's book. That component of great companies was what Collins called a BHAG.[1]

A BHAG is a Big, Hairy, Audacious Goal. It's a visionary dream that is believed in fully by the company's board and management but on the surface seems almost impossible to achieve. It's a dream so grand, so massive, and so out of the box that it requires every employee's belief and best efforts for the company to have any chance of making it a reality. It's a goal that outlasts the life of the original leader. It is bigger than any one person and is so enthralling and all-encompassing that it easily survives the transition from one leader to another. Great companies, said Collins, have BHAGs that enable the company to move seamlessly from one generation of leaders to the next. The company becomes concerned with its grand goals, not the personality or leadership style of its current president or CEO.

For example, in 1961 President John F. Kennedy painted a picture of our nation's future that included space exploration. He boldly called on the government to allocate enough resources to put a man on the moon by the end of the decade. The country embraced Kennedy's challenge, the government rallied to his cause, and in 1969 Neil Armstrong became the first man to

> The history of Christianity has been written through prayers that dared to believe God for the impossible.

walk on the moon. Kennedy's vision lasted way beyond his untimely death in 1963. That's a BHAG.

I'd like to borrow from Jim Collins's language and introduce you to the concept of BHAPs—Big, Hairy, Audacious Prayers. A BHAP is the kind of prayer that takes your breath away. It's a vision so God-sized, so humanly impossible, and yet so utterly appealing that it totally consumes you—and it drives you to your knees in prayer. BHAPs are not only biblical, they're precisely the kind of prayers that Jesus exhorted us to pray.

In Acts 1, Jesus gave his disciples a vision and an assignment to be his witnesses all over the world. Then, before he ascended into heaven, he basically said, "Stay tuned." They were left with their Master's command to spread his message around the world still ringing in their ears. Nothing could have been more impossible. Nothing could have seemed so ludicrous. And so they prayed. The vision they had from Christ drove them to an upper room where they prayed and waited for God to come through. That was BHAP praying. Ten days later, God poured out his Spirit on them, and the rest, as they say, is history.

It was BHAP praying in Acts 4 when the disciples asked God for boldness and courage in the face of persecution instead of deliverance from it. It was BHAP praying in Acts 9 when Peter prayed for Dorcas to be brought back to life. It was BHAP praying in Acts 12 when the church prayed all night for Peter's release from prison. And in every case, God came through with boldness, deliverance, and life that the disciples could never have mustered on their own. That's the power of big, hairy, audacious praying: it tends to solicit big, hairy, audacious answers from God. The history of Christianity has been written through prayers that dared to believe God for the impossible.

And Jesus Said, "Go for It!"

It might be easy to think that we're misinterpreting this concept if there were only one or two vague verses in the Bible about making big asks of God. But that's not the reality. If anything, the biblical call to pray big is an open-and-shut case. Let's consider some of the Bible's sweeping promises on prayer in the Old Testament.

To a nation on the eve of exile, to a nation that had rejected God and would lose its national heritage, the Lord still promised, "Call to me and I will answer you and tell you great and unsearchable things you do not know" (Jer. 33:3). In other words, God simply said, "Hey, people, go ahead and think of the biggest and boldest prayers you can pray. Go ahead and call them out to me, because there is no way you're ever going to drain my resources. You have no idea how much I can still do for you."

Through the prophet Isaiah, God declared, "Then you will call, and the LORD will answer; you will cry for help, and he will say: Here am I" (Isa. 58:9). He also promised, "Surely the arm of the LORD is not too short to save, nor his ear too dull to hear" (Isa. 59:1). And God instructed Israel's intercessors, "I have posted watchmen on your walls, O Jerusalem; they will never be silent day or night. You who call on the LORD, give yourselves no rest, and give him no rest till he establishes Jerusalem and makes her the praise of the earth" (Isa. 62:6–7). I love that promise and have prayed it on countless occasions. It's like God is saying, "I want you to bombard heaven with your prayers. Don't let up until I come through in every last detail!"

Through the prophet Joel, long before the advent of Christ and the event of the cross, God promised that "everyone who calls on the name of the LORD will be saved" (Joel 2:32). God taught that through the humble prayer of the contrite sinner, he would bring salvation to his people. Can you think of a bigger ask we can make of God? Is there any bolder request we can make of a holy God than to save an unholy sinner? And yet there it is, plastered all over the pages of the Old Testament. God wants to and will answer our prayers for deliverance. As God promised through Jeremiah, "Then you will call upon me and come and pray to me, and I will listen to you. You will seek me and find me when you seek me with all your heart" (Jer. 29:12–13).

In the New Testament, the centuries-old promises of God become stunningly urgent and clear in the teachings of Christ. Jesus could not have been more emphatic about his belief in prayer or our ability to seek breathtaking answers from God. Simply put, there is no greater advocate of big prayer in the Bible than Jesus. Consider just a few of the claims Jesus made about prayer.

> But when you pray, go into your room, close the door and pray to your Father, who is unseen. Then your Father, who sees what is done in secret, will reward you.
>
> Matthew 6:6

> Ask and it will be given to you; seek and you will find; knock and the door will be opened to you. For everyone who asks receives; he who seeks finds; and to him who knocks, the door will be opened.
>
> Matthew 7:7–8

Again, I tell you that if two of you on earth agree about anything you ask for, it will be done for you by my Father in heaven. For where two or three come together in my name, there am I with them.

Matthew 18:19–20

And all things you ask in prayer, believing, you will receive.

Matthew 21:22 NASB

And I will do whatever you ask in my name, so that the Son may bring glory to the Father. You may ask me for anything in my name, and I will do it.

John 14:13–14

If you remain in me and my words remain in you, ask whatever you wish, and it will be given you.

John 15:7

You did not choose me, but I chose you and appointed you to go and bear fruit—fruit that will last. Then the Father will give you whatever you ask in my name.

John 15:16

In that day you will no longer ask me anything. I tell you the truth, my Father will give you whatever you ask in my name. Until now you have not asked for anything in my name. Ask and you will receive, and your joy will be complete.

John 16:23–24

In his teachings on prayer, Jesus contrasted God and a wicked judge. He taught that they were exact opposites in the way they responded to needy people. The only reason the judge gave justice to a poor widow was because she nearly pestered him to death. God, on the other hand, looks for chances to answer our prayers and to come through for his followers (see Luke 18:1–8). Jesus taught that God was like a loving father who loves to give the very best gifts to his children (see Matt. 7:9–11). Jesus also told his disciples that he had given them the keys to heaven and that they could actually unlock the power of heaven with their prayers (see Matt. 16:19). Finally, Jesus said that with even the smallest amounts of faith—faith as small as a single piece of salt or fleck of pepper—they could move mountains (see Matt. 17:20–21).

Do you see a theme developing here? Could Jesus have been any more deliberate in his exhortations for us to seek huge things from God? He wants us to ask God for his very best.

Why do you suppose Jesus spoke almost to the point of redundancy about prayer? Why was he so emphatic about it? Jesus knew that his disciples' success depended on prayer and that they would never see any impact for the kingdom without it. He knew the kind of supernatural power that prayer would make available to them. He also knew that his church would never be built without it. In short, Jesus expected his disciples to pray.

He expects the same of us. Are you praying BHAPs? Do you regularly go before God seeking kingdom-level answers? Do your prayers require the best of God? As a follower of Christ, you need to know that you're on solid biblical ground when you're seeking miraculous things from God. You also need to know that all the divine power of the Creator of the universe stands ready to move when you pray.

BHAP Benefits

Before you write off BHAPs as only for the spiritually elite or only for those who have the gift of intercession, I'd like you to consider something. Did you know that God has gifted you with the Holy Spirit so you can effectively ask and receive dramatic things from him? BHAP praying is part and parcel of being a fruit-bearing disciple. Here are just a few good reasons for you to be constantly seeking big things from God.

- **BHAPs humble you.** There's nothing like a breathtaking prayer request to squash your pride. When you're begging God for a spouse to be saved, for a cancerous tumor to be removed, for a shattered relationship to be miraculously restored, or for finances to be supernaturally provided, it's hard to be cocky before him. Making such lofty requests really does give you a proper perspective before the one from whom you are seeking answers.

- **BHAPs make you dependent on God.** When you're praying for the impossible, you find out in a hurry where your strength really lies. When the church in Acts 12 was praying for Peter's release from prison, they knew better than to rush out and try to break Peter out of jail. They would have had no chance against Herod's forces. All they could do was pray. The rest was up to God. And that is precisely where kingdom work gets done. When all you can do is pray and wait on God, you're a prime candidate for a kingdom-level miracle.

- **BHAPs drive you to the Bible.** If you're asking God to move a mountain for you, be sure that you're on solid biblical ground. BHAPs can be given in confidence only when you know that the Bible has endorsed your asking. Prayers for healing, forgiveness, restoration, and vision require you to know God's Word. That's why BHAP praying is so good for you. It makes you get into the Bible.

- **BHAPs increase your faith.** When you venture out and make a big ask of God, faith is required. Then, when God comes through, faith increases. The entire exercise of BHAP praying is one big spiritual faith builder. When you repeatedly go before God with kingdom-sized requests, you'll see that your hope and confidence in God's provision increase with every foray into his holy presence. Praying big prayers and seeing God's even bigger answers grow your faith.

- **BHAPs enlist you in kingdom pursuits.** Spiritual walls are torn down in prayer. Captives are set free through prayer. Mountains are blown away by prayer. The kingdom is built one prayer at a time. Prayer is indeed the fuel of God's kingdom. But prayer never happens in a vacuum. Prayers don't fall off a prayer tree. Prayer happens only when there is a pray-er. The person who prays becomes a player in the highest-stakes game in all of history. Praying people disengage from the temporal to focus on the eternal. They set aside earthly desires to seek heavenly ones. And, through the mechanism of prayer, they become enlisted warriors in the battle of the ages. BHAP praying isn't just a pastime or hobby for the truly spiritually minded. It's the tool of choice for true kingdom builders.

Discovering Your BHAPs

Perhaps as you've been reading, you've already noted some big, hairy, audacious requests that you're making of God. You're praying for an addiction to be broken or for a friend's business to be successful. You're praying for an atheist professor to find Christ or for God to change the heart of a national leader. Maybe you're praying for the return of a prodigal son, or perhaps you're asking God for a miraculous physical healing. Whatever the case, if you're in the business of praying BHAPs, you already know it.

But maybe you've realized that you're not making sufficient asks of God. You've realized that you don't have any real BHAPs. You've recognized that you're stuck at the *God, bless Tom* level of praying. Are you ready to start asking for bigger things? Maybe you're wondering, *How do I know what to pray for? How do I find the right BHAP to set before God?* Here are some simple suggestions.

Examine your concerns. This isn't difficult. Just start with the areas that you worry or fret over the most. Are you worried about your marriage, your career, a friend's salvation? Then why not make it a BHAP? Turn your fears and worries into big asks of God. Also, consider your passions. What areas would you most like to impact or most like to see changed in your world? Turn them into BHAPs.

I pray just about every day for my hometown of Austin to be known around the world as a God-fearing city. I love Austin and am saddened by the spiritual confusion that reigns there. But all my sadness and worrying won't help the city. So several years ago, along with starting a church to help Austinites find Christ, I started praying some very specific biblical promises for my hometown. Every one of them was a BHAP. And I'm still asking Jesus to do really big things in a city that I know he loves and died for. That's BHAP praying.

Find verses of the Bible that state what you want God to do. I gave up a long time ago on trying to find creative and persuasive language to use with God. Now I just pray what he's already said he wants and is willing to do. The Bible is an incredible source of BHAP promises. Once you've identified your passion or concern areas,

Pray Big

34

start combing the Scriptures for verses that clearly state your desires.

Another **BHAP** I pray nearly every day is for five thousand believing men to fill our church. Acts 4:4 says, "Many who heard the message believed, and the number of men grew to about five thousand." That "five thousand [men]" phrase appears more than once in the New Testament.

One day I felt the Spirit nudge me to start praying for five thousand believing, praying men in our church. Can you imagine the impact a church of five thousand spiritual warring men could have on a city? Today in our church, we're still a long way from having five thousand of anything, so that's a very outrageous prayer. But you can still find the phrase "five thousand men" written on many of the pages of my Bible.

Do you want wayward children to come home? Then remind God of his love for prodigals (see Luke 15:11–24). Do you long to see someone under extreme spiritual oppression liberated? Then pray that Jesus will do for them what he did for spiritually oppressed people in the Gospels (see Luke 8:26–39). Are you unable to forgive someone who has wronged you? Pray for the kind of heart that Jesus had for his enemies (see Luke 23:34). The Bible is loaded with ready-made prayers to help you express your BHAPs to God. Become a student of the Bible and learn how to mine the treasures of its promises.

Pray. Don't just come up with BHAPs for your own entertainment. Have the spiritual gumption to pray them! Where would Zechariah and Elizabeth have been if they had only wished for a child? What if they had talked about BHAPs and read about them in the Hebrew Scriptures but never got around to asking God for their own BHAP? At some point, if we're really serious about securing miraculous things from God, we've got to be equally serious about asking him for them.

Tenacity is a critical word to describe BHAP praying. If you're going to secure big things from God in prayer, then you'd better be willing to keep after it until he comes through. Drive-by praying and miraculous answers rarely go together.

> If we're really serious about securing miraculous things from God, we've got to be equally serious about asking him for them.

Remember the verse from Isaiah we looked at a little earlier in this chapter: "I have posted watchmen on your walls, O Jerusalem; they will never be silent day or night. You who call on the LORD, give yourselves no rest, and give him no rest till he establishes Jerusalem and makes her the praise of the earth" (Isa. 62:6–7). God's command there is to never be silent. He wants us to persistently seek him until he answers. He says that we are to give him no rest. That means that every day, every time we go before God, we need to remind him of our needs and his promises. Tell God that you are completely serious about securing his answer. Tell him that you will not be silent until he moves in the situation for which you're praying. Show God that you're willing to pray and wait until he comes through just like he promised.

I use my Bible as my prayer guide. It's filled with literally hundreds of names and needs that I take before God regularly. Some of the same names and needs appear on nearly every page. They are there to remind me not to miss a day praying for Mike's salvation or Austin's revival or our church's financial provision. Are you doing that? Are you being tenacious in your prayers? Don't quit! You may be just one prayer away from a huge breakthrough. Stay at it.

We Missed It by Only a Mile

When our church was very small and only a few years old, our leadership decided that we needed to start praying about land. We were leasing a small office facility at the time, and even though we were several years away from being in a position to purchase anything, we knew that we needed to start praying about our permanent location in Austin. Being from Austin, I had a pretty good idea of the part of town we might look at.

The hill country west of Austin is known for its beautiful vistas, lake access, gorgeous oak trees, and, of course, high prices. It also represents the fastest-growing corridor in our city. On a major highway that runs through the hills, there is a locally famous stretch of land known as Tumbleweed Hill. It used to be home to the Tumbleweed Restaurant, a steak place that sat atop the hill with a breathtaking view of the nearby valley. It was an Austin landmark. The restaurant tract was a narrow ten acres and was for sale at the time we started looking for land. It didn't take too much dreaming on our part to set our sights on the Tumbleweed Restaurant site.

I remember quite clearly the day in the mid-1990s when I drove out to the Tumbleweed site with the rest of the church staff. We stood on the foundation where the old restaurant used to be, looked at the amazing views around us, and watched as hundreds of cars whizzed by. Even though the site was very narrow, we still couldn't think of a better location for a church trying to impact Austin. It was perfect.

On that day, the four of us circled up, joined hands, and prayed. We asked God to put us on that piece of land. We told him why we wanted it and why we thought it made sense for our church. That, my friends, was serious BHAP praying, because we had few assets, no money to speak of, and no connections to help us shortcut our way onto that land. But we felt like that was where we were supposed to be, so we prayed, *God, give us this land.*

We missed it by a mile, literally. A mile down the road, just off the main thoroughfare, was some property we knew nothing about. Two adjacent pieces of land totaling sixty acres were just becoming available. They were relatively undeveloped, loaded with huge oak trees, and right in the middle of one of the fastest-growing areas of Austin. The only thing different was the view. The two tracts didn't offer views of the neighboring valley like Tumbleweed Hill did. They offered views of the entire city and all the neighboring valleys! In fact, the tracts sit on the highest geographical point in the city of Austin.

Today that land is the home of Austin Christian Fellowship, the church I pastor. Over the next few years, after we prayed for the Tumbleweed site, God worked through a series of amazing and unlikely circumstances, providing one miracle after another to put us on that land.

We had prayed a BHAP and dared to believe that God had great things in mind for his church. Our prayers apparently weren't big, hairy, and audacious enough, because God far exceeded what we had asked for. I'm so glad he did.

Ladies and Gentlemen, Start Your BHAPing

What's stopping you from making some big asks of God? What mountain needs moving in your life? What problem needs solving? What do you wish God would do in your life, your family, your church, your city, or your nation? Start praying your BHAPs! God wants you to ask him. And if you're wrong, if your BHAP is way off course, trust that God will redirect you. Chances are that your BHAP may be only part of what he wants to do for you. So get to it.

Discussion Questions

1. Why do you think God included so many promises about prayer in the Bible? Why is prayer so important to God?
2. The Bible portrays God as ready and eager to answer your prayers. Is that different from how you think God feels about your prayers? If so, how?
3. What concerns do you have today that you could easily turn into BHAPs?
4. What is the biggest, God-sized request you're making of God currently?
5. What BHAP have you been afraid to ask God? Why have you hesitated?
6. In light of what you've learned in this chapter, how will your prayers be different? What BHAPs will you start giving to God that you haven't previously?

CHECKBOOKS, CAR KEYS, AND AXHEADS

Pinpoint Praying for Little Things

Do not be anxious about anything, but in everything, by prayer and petition, with thanksgiving, present your requests to God.

Philippians 4:6

*D*ear God, I know you can see my checkbook. Please show me where I left it.

Things were not going well. My wife had sent me down to our neighborhood bank to open a checking account. I drove to the bank in my truck and spent a half hour at the accounts desk signing papers and entering passwords. Finally the perky teller shook my hand, handed me my new checkbook and paperwork, congratulated me on my choice of banks, and sent me on my way. Just before I drove off, I noticed that I didn't have the checkbook. Figuring I'd left it at the accounts desk, I went back inside. It wasn't there. The perky teller assured me that I hadn't left it at the desk. So I retraced my steps. No checkbook. I scoured every inch of the fifty feet between the bank's front door and my truck. I looked in the gutter by my parking place; I looked under my truck; I looked under the cars next to my truck. I looked in my pockets, in my pants and shirt, everywhere. No checkbook. Then I tore the truck apart, looking in the glove compartment, under the mats, between the seats, behind the visors. Finally I mumbled, *God, show me where I left the checkbook.* No checkbook.

I swallowed my pride, walked back into the bank, sat down at the same desk, and talked to the same perky teller. I had to close the account I'd opened only an hour before and then open another account with different paperwork and new passwords. Then the same perky teller shook my hand, handed me my new checkbook and paperwork, congratulated me on my choice of banks, and sent me on my way—again. This time I made it to the car with the checkbook. As I drove home, I wondered how I would explain to my wife why it took me two hours to open a checking account.

Fast forward three months. I walked down our driveway to my truck to run an errand. I realized when I sat down that I didn't have my keys. Thinking I'd left them in the house, I went back inside. No car keys. I checked the twenty feet between our back door and my truck, thinking I might have dropped them. I looked in my pockets and searched my briefcase. I prayed, and then I tore the truck apart looking for those keys. I never found them.

The good news is I found my checkbook—in my truck!

God Is in the Details

Philippians 4:6 instructs us to pray about everything. If Paul had wanted us to limit our praying to everything *big*, he certainly would have told us. But he tells us to pray about *everything*. For those of us who are in the habit of losing our checkbooks and car keys, that's great news.

God is as interested in your small, seemingly insignificant requests as he is your kingdom-level, life-changing needs. God's interest in your prayers isn't dependent upon their relative kingdom weightiness. It's based on his love for and interest in you.

Let's consider a little-known story from 2 Kings 6:1–7 that demonstrates this truth. The prophet Elisha had a group of young men he was mentoring and training—sort of a prophets' training school. Any preparatory course offered by Elisha was the hottest ticket in town if you were a prophet in training. Elisha had been trained by none other than Elijah, arguably the greatest prophet in Israel's history.

The group of young men talked Elisha into joining them in a construction project on the banks of the Jordan River. They wanted to build a house where they could live in community, study under Elisha, and develop their prophetic skills.

While the men worked near the river, cutting down trees to be used for making the house, an iron axhead flew off its handle. It splashed into the Jordan and sank deep to its bottom. The young man using the ax was visibly upset. He confided in Elisha that the ax was not his. He'd borrowed it, and he felt bad about the loss.

> God is as interested in your small, seemingly insignificant requests as he is your kingdom-level, life-changing needs.

43

An ax was a valuable tool in an agrarian society. The young man had no doubt promised to return the tool in good shape. Its loss would be costly to both the young prophet and its owner. So he brought the need to Elisha in hopes that he might somehow help.

Obviously, a lost axhead doesn't register as a major crisis on the "need" scale. It doesn't seem nearly as important as the true prophetic work for which these men were training. How could a lost axhead merit the attention of a prophet when there were widows' sons to be raised, droughts to be ended, rivers to be parted, and evil kings to be rebuked? But while this problem might not have been a big deal to the other men in his community, it was a major issue to the young prophet. And that was all the wise and godly Elisha needed to know.

He asked the young man where the axhead had fallen into the water. Then Elisha took a branch and dropped it into the water at that spot. After just a brief moment, the axhead floated to the surface. The young man was able to retrieve the axhead, complete his work, and return the borrowed ax to its owner.

It's a simple story, one that takes up only seven verses in the entire Old Testament. In the broad scheme of Israel's history, the story has no apparent impact. It does show Elisha's power as a prophet, but many other stories show his power in much more dramatic and significant ways. So why would the biblical writer include this story? Why did the Holy Spirit think it necessary to include a story about a floating iron axhead?

What Would You Have Done?

Let's stop and think for a minute. In your world as a Christ-follower, does a broken garden tool merit prayer?

> When something breaks your heart—large or small—it isn't going to escape God's attention.

How about a friend's missing keys or your child's sick hamster? If you borrowed a tool from a neighbor and accidentally broke or lost it, would you take the problem to God in prayer? Probably not. Our fast-paced world doesn't typically reserve prayer time for such "trivial" matters. We'd most likely rush off to Home Depot, buy a replacement, throw in a Starbucks gift certificate, and beg forgiveness. The whole episode would be over as quickly as it started. Why is that? Is it because we simply don't have time or don't think it's appropriate to pray about small things? Or is it because we don't think God gives a rip about something as noneternal as a neighbor's broken tool?

Let's go back to those few verses in 2 Kings and ask again why God might have wanted them included in the Bible. Maybe God wanted us to know that his power is available to us in all types of situations. Perhaps he wanted to show us that he is concerned about all our needs, regardless of how trivial or insignificant they may seem. Maybe one of the points of this story is that God cares for us for our own sake—not for what we can do for him, not for what we bring to the kingdom table, and not for the level of eternal impact we may have. After much meditation and thought about this story, I'm convinced that is exactly what God is trying to say.

This story doesn't just confirm that Elisha was a prophet of the highest order; it also shows us where God's priorities lie. Simply stated, God's priority is you. He created you, loves you, and has a plan for you. When something breaks your heart—large or small—it isn't going to escape God's attention. God included this story in his Word so that we'd be encouraged to bring every need we have to him, not just those that seem destined to make kingdom headlines. In short, God wants you to talk to him about everything, even your missing car keys.

Debunking Your God Myths

If we're going to have any confidence approaching God about seemingly little things, then we'd better shed some of the extra pounds that we may have attached to our image of God over the years. Let's take a look at some commonly held beliefs about God that would cause us to think that he's uninterested in our "little" prayers.

God's too busy. It may seem that God is much too hard at work rebuking the devil, chasing off demons, and managing the entire angelic realm—not to mention keeping the universe and all its corresponding physical laws in place—to have time to hear your tiny request. Plus, he's got billions of people simultaneously talking to him in thousands of different languages. Surely a prayer for a missing checkbook would be lost in the shuffle of the great prayer lottery.

In reality, however, "busy" is something God has never experienced. It's a human characteristic. We're finite, with limited resources, abilities, and time. When we try to cram too much of anything into our time and resource pools, we experience "busy." God never does. He has infinite resources and abilities, and time is something he created. He can't get stressed or over-committed. Listening to the prayers of billions of people isn't work to God. He has all the time and energy required to hear each of us and respond singularly to every request.

My prayer is too insignificant to merit God's attention. Another popular God myth is that only the seriously important or ultimately eternal need is worthy of God's focus and energy. God's attention is merited only when the stakes are eternally high. Curing the sick, finding a missing child, or saving a lost soul are the types of things we should take before God. Our more trivial and noneternal matters simply don't merit the heavenly interest of a holy God. So if you have a missing kitten, if you really need to pass that geometry quiz, or if your car won't start and you're late for a meeting, you needn't bother to pray about it. Such insignificant matters never reach God's ears. They simply don't matter in eternity.

Have you ever felt that way? You wanted to pray about something that was important to you, even though it would never register on God's heavenly Richter scale. But you kept your need to yourself simply because you thought there was no way it could matter to God. You chose worry over prayer, stress over hope, and defeat over victory because you believed God simply wouldn't respond to something so trivial.

Why did God raise the missing axhead? Because it mattered to one of his children. The power of prayer lies in the fact that it's based on a relationship, not on the weight of what's being asked. All prayer matters to God because it flows from the heart of someone he created and loves dearly.

The biblical writers went out of their way to paint a picture of God as the perfect dad. In the same way a loving father is interested in the tiniest need of his child, the perfect God is even more attuned to the tiniest needs of his children. Jesus said that a sparrow couldn't fall to the ground without the Father's noticing. If that's the case, then surely God has the patience and time for your concerns, even though they may not seem to have any real eternal impact. Check out the promises about answered prayer in the New Testament. You won't find one that says your prayer has to pass God's significance test before he'll be willing to hear it. It's significant to God because it's significant to you. Your prayer matters to God because you do.

Praying about little things is selfish. Perhaps you've heard, "How can you pray for God to give you a parking place downtown when there are Christians in China being persecuted for their faith?" Or "How selfish can you be? You're asking God to help you lose ten pounds when there are children in Africa dying of malnutrition." To some degree, I'm tempted to agree with such reasoning.

On the surface, it does seem selfish for me to pray about my upcoming meeting with my stockbroker—that I might have wisdom to invest my resources well—when there are people across town who will sleep on the streets tonight. But actually, there is much to be gained by my dialogue with God over even the most trivial of matters. Is it selfish when we ask God to bless the food we're about to eat? Is a truck driver being selfish when he or she prays for safety at the beginning of a long road trip? Is a student praying selfishly when he or she asks God for a fresh mind and a high retention capacity before studying for a major exam? Not according to the New Testament. The apostle Paul exhorted Christians to pray without ceasing (see 1 Thess. 5:17). That means that he wanted prayer to be as natural to us as breathing. You shouldn't have to segregate your big, important prayers from your smaller ones. They're all important to God.

If we believe that God is able to work out all things—even small ones—for his good purpose and his glory, then of course we should pray about even the tiniest of matters. Your request for God's work in your financial investments, in the food you're about to eat, and in your study habits may be just the thing he can use to build his kingdom in your life.

Grow Up and Pray like a Child

Frequently Jesus was asked what the kingdom of God would be like. He came preaching about the kingdom of God, and he promised to build it. That no doubt aroused much curiosity in his audience as they were filled with political hopes for a glorified new Israel. People frequently asked Jesus what his vision for God's kingdom was. They wanted to know who the true power players would be. They were curious if their own hopes and dreams for influence in God's kingdom would be fulfilled.

So once, after being asked about God's kingdom, Jesus decided to give his audience an object lesson. He took a child—say, a seven-year-old—and had him stand before the crowd. Then he basically said, "If you want to know what life is like in God's kingdom, look at this child. If you want to know who the real power brokers are in God's kingdom, look at the children. If you're curious about how to be a mover and shaker on a kingdom level, start acting, thinking, and asking like a little child. The kingdom of God belongs to people who are just like them." (See Matt. 18:1–4 and Mark 10:15.)

I love those verses. They assure me that sophistication isn't required when dealing with God. Rather, the wonderful childlike attributes of naïveté, innocence, curiosity, unquestioning trust, and bold asking are the way and rule in God's family. That encourages me to "go for it" when I approach God in prayer. There will be times when I pray with gut-wrenching earnestness for a troubled marriage to be saved. And there will be times

Checkbooks, Car Keys, and Axheads

49

when I'll ask God to help me find my child's missing baseball. The Scriptures promise me that both prayers are things that God can use to draw me to himself, to show me his glory, to honor himself through me, and to teach me his ways.

Don't Sweat the Small Stuff—Pray about It!

Hopefully, by now you're starting to believe that God isn't put out when you pray about the small stuff. You've considered some of those awesome promises and teachings in God's Word, and you're beginning to understand that he really does care about the little details of your life. But perhaps you're not convinced that such praying is worth it for you. Many people don't pray about the little things because they feel they're not worth *their* time. They reserve prayer for those high and mighty occasions when they've exhausted every possible human solution and prayer is all that's left to them. The truth is that they really don't want to invest prayer energy in things of seemingly little significance. And they're missing spiritual blessings as a result.

Prayer has unbelievable benefits to us, even when we're just praying about a lost set of car keys. Let's take a look at some of the advantages of incorporating prayer into even the smallest details of our lives.

Praying for the little things teaches you to depend on God. In kingdom matters, we're not nearly as independent as we'd like to think. In fact, Jesus taught that the sum total of our ability to have kingdom impact outside of his assistance was a big, whopping zero. In John 15:5, Jesus said that apart from him we could do nothing. In other words, we can do nothing by ourselves that has any real spiritual significance. Now, it's true that I can still do many things without Jesus. I can sin, struggle, worry, and try really hard to be good and still fail without Jesus. But what I can't do without Jesus is live a godly life, bear spiritual fruit, and have lasting eternal impact. Those types of things require Jesus's fullness and presence in my life.

When I'm praying, I'm acknowledging my dependence on God. I'm deliberately unplugging from my earthly and human sources of strength and choosing rather to plug in to God's holy and infinite source. Prayer is an all-out declaration of dependence. When you choose to seek God's leadership, direction, and provision for something as seemingly insignificant as a parking place, the right wording of a letter, or what clothes to wear to the office, you're acknowledging that you want and need God's direction in every aspect of your day. You're inviting Jesus to rule and reign as Lord over every last detail of your life. That's pinpoint praying that pleases God. That's prayer that teaches you how to depend on him in everything.

Since prayer is communion and dialogue with God, praying for little things teaches you to enjoy his presence. The benefit of praying isn't primarily the answer we get from God; it's the pleasure of actually being with God in the asking. Prayer is one of the few Christian disciplines that can safely be described as an end in itself. In those holy moments of prayer, you encounter the reality of a holy God. At the point you discover God's presence in prayer, the matter for which you're seeking him becomes secondary. God's presence, even more than God's blessing, becomes the goal of prayer.

If I limit my prayers to just the big, dramatic things in my life, I miss hundreds of opportunities every day for sweet communion with God.

If I limit my prayers to just the big, dramatic things in my

Checkbooks, Car Keys, and Axheads

life, I miss hundreds of opportunities every day for sweet communion with God. But if I bring prayer down to the missing-axhead level, I invite God's presence into the most remote details of my life.

So go ahead and talk to God while you're writing a check to the dry cleaner. Pray for the salesperson behind the counter and ask God to reveal himself to him or her. When you meet with a co-worker, even if it's just a routine meeting, pray beforehand. Ask God to humble you and to exalt himself through you in the meeting. Pray that your co-worker will see God's glory in you. And the next time you're seated at a café, reading a menu, ask God what you should order. Now, that's a dangerous prayer! Think how your diet might change if you prayed about it. Praying over your menu choices acknowledges that even the act of eating is a gift from God and invites him into your dining setting. It can turn a seemingly routine meal into an occasion for communion with God.

Seeking God in the little things increases your gratitude and offers perspective. There are many people in the world whose lives are marked with a level of pain and grief that I can't comprehend. I don't know what it's like to not know where my next meal is coming from. I've never been the victim of a violent crime. I'm not the survivor of a life-threatening illness. I've never lived through a natural disaster. Many in the world around me have.

Beyond that, I live in a country that allows me to worship freely. Recently our church hosted some refugees from the underground church in China. They came to our midweek service to share about God's work in the midst of severe persecution of the Chinese church. I'll never forget the reactions of the Chinese believers as they walked into our auditorium and heard singing and worshiping. The room was filled with praise that was lovingly and freely expressed. One of the Chinese guests commented to me that she hadn't quite gotten used to the volume levels of worship in Western churches. In the home churches in China, Christians can't sing loudly. They worship in secret and literally have to whisper their prayers and praises for fear of being discovered and arrested. I think about that just about every time I belt out a loud song of blessing to God. I also think about those millions of persecuted Chinese believers every time I pray for a missing set of car keys. When I think of the needs of my persecuted brothers and sisters, the fact that I even have a car humbles me. Praying for little things reminds me of just how blessed I really am; it keeps everything in proper perspective.

So go ahead and seek God about the tiniest details of your life. It'll be good for you too. You'll thank him that, at least at that moment, your concerns aren't more significant.

You should pray for little things, because they often turn into big things. When God floated that ax-head, he did much more than just help a young man return a borrowed tool to his neighbor. He validated Elisha's ministry and showed those young prophets that his power was available to them as well. Imagine the courage, confidence, and spiritual momentum that developed in that camp after the axhead miracle.

Praying for little things opens you up to God's power. It also gives him the opportunity to turn your tiny prayer into a major God event.

Let me tell you a story that illustrates this truth. Years ago when I was quite young and very inexperienced in ministry, I helped to start a small church a block or two from where I lived in north Austin. My wife, Susie, and I were without children, and we both had lots of time to devote to each other and to our ministry. One day when I was making the short drive to my office, I prayed about my poor evangelism habits. I knew I wasn't sharing Christ as frequently as I needed to. I prayed the simple pinpoint prayer that God would give me more opportunities to share my faith with others.

Moments later, as I pulled into the church parking lot, I was met by a member of our youth group. His name was Todd, and he was seventeen and came from a tough family situation. He attended a school in Austin for kids who were too rough and unruly to be placed in regular classes. His car wouldn't start, so he'd walked to the church in hopes of bumming a ride to school from one of our staff members. (Since I was the only staff member, that would be me.) I had been concerned for Todd for a long time and felt a lot of compassion for him. I was more than happy to take him to school.

We were late to Todd's first class, so he asked me to walk him in and vouch for his story to his teacher. The minute we walked into his class, Todd was met by a chorus of jeers and harassing comments from his classmates about his tardiness. When they saw me, they began to joke that I was his parole officer. Clearly without thinking, Todd blurted out, "He's my pastor!" I think Todd believed that somehow a pastor would merit more respect from this rowdy crowd, but he was wrong. Wild and raucous laughter now greeted us both. I really just wanted to clear Todd with the teacher and make a quick getaway. This was no longer my idea of a productive way to spend a morning.

I introduced myself to the teacher and explained why Todd was late. As I turned to leave, one of the kids yelled out, "Hey, preacher, what do you guys believe at your church, anyway?"

I need to explain that this wasn't said in a particularly respectful fashion. It didn't sound like a genuine inquiry from a true spiritual seeker. The kid's tone of voice sounded like he was really saying, "Hey, dude, surely you don't really believe any of that stupid religious stuff! What a waste of time!" The cynicism and sarcasm were practically dripping off his words. I had clearly been challenged.

Knowing I was in a public school, in a class filled with troubled seventeen-year-olds, and in very hostile territory, I turned and looked at the teacher for some sort of sign. If anything, she seemed amused by the situation. She simply nodded, smiled, and motioned with her head toward the class. It was as if she was saying, "Hey, if you can handle it, go for it." Suddenly I had been granted a captive audience.

I sat down on a desk, and for the next forty-five minutes, I shared with the class and answered questions about the Christian faith. I was amazed at how the mood of the group turned from wild and skeptical to attentive and serious in just a few minutes. They had a genuine interest in knowing what Christians claimed and what bearing the teachings of Jesus might have on their lives. It appeared that no Christian had ever taken the time to clearly explain what he or she believed to them.

I spent the entire period with the class. When I left, they actually thanked me for my time. The teacher, who still had not said a word, just kept smiling.

I drove away from the school that day with huge goose bumps on my arms, completely overwhelmed by what had just taken place. At that point in my Christian life, it was one of the most exhilarating kingdom experiences I'd ever had. I imagine I felt just like those young prophets did when they saw that floating axhead. I hate to admit this, but it was much later in the day before I remembered what I'd prayed just before I ran into Todd.

I've seen similar scenarios played out hundreds of times in the lives of other Christ-followers. A Christian offers up a simple prayer about something quite small and seemingly unimportant. And before he or she knows it, God has answered the prayer in a huge, astounding, kingdom-impacting way.

What Are You Waiting For?

God has given us overwhelming evidence of his desire to answer our prayers. He's loaded his Word with hundreds of promises, each assuring us that he will come through when we pray. Jesus taught us that God is the great promise keeper, and he loves to answer our prayers. Further, not one time does God establish a minimum significance requirement for our requests to merit his attention.

Start today, right now, taking every need, every choice, every concern, every idea, every fear, every hope, every worry, and every dream—regardless of how small you may think it is—to God. Don't leave out anything. Every prayer you pray is a chance for you to get to know God more, to experience his wonderful presence, and to allow him to show himself strong on your behalf.

Discussion Questions

1. Okay, be honest: when was the last time you prayed for something really small and seemingly insignificant, like a parking place? What happened?
2. What does the account of God raising the missing axhead tell you about how he views your most basic, everyday needs?
3. Have you ever felt selfish for praying for your little needs? What does the Bible say about how God views your littlest needs?

4. Praying for little things makes you more dependent on God. How do your current prayer habits reflect your level of dependency on God?
5. How might your life change if you started praying for even the tiniest details in your life?
6. After reading this chapter, how will your prayers be different?

4

FROM SPIRITUALLY DEAD TO SPIRITUAL SERVANT

Pinpoint Praying for Unbelievers

Brothers, my heart's desire and prayer to God for the Israelites is that they may be saved.

Romans 10:1

I grew up going to church, and I believed that following the Ten Commandments and being a good person was all I really needed to do to get to heaven. It wasn't until a friend told me some years back that that's not what being a Christian is all about. I then realized I had spiritual work to do. However, I continued on my merry way because it was way easier than thinking about Jesus. Over the years, I went to a few different churches, but I never felt that I belonged.

This is what Stephanie Morton of Austin wrote in the testimony she shared at her baptism.

If you ever met Stephanie, it would be easy to be impressed. She's a tall, willowy beauty with a gentle way about her. She has a smile that can light up a dark room. Stephanie is married to a great man and is raising three wonderful boys. In looking at her, you would be tempted to think that she has it all. From an earthly standpoint, she does. She is alive and vibrant and happy.

But for a long time, Stephanie, along with many others just like her, still had a great spiritual need. Her soul was asleep. The most beautiful thing about her—her human spirit—had yet to be made fully alive by God. She was in a perpetual state of spiritual slumber. Stephanie knew she had a need, but she wasn't able to articulate it. What she ultimately needed was a spiritual Prince Charming to come and rouse her sleeping soul. Specifically, she needed Jesus to awaken her into a relationship with him.

Stephanie showed up at a Bible study our church was offering for spiritual skeptics. She shared some of her religious and church experiences growing up and expressed more doubts about Christianity than anything else. But she was open and willing to do any studying required to reach her own conclusions about Christ. I immediately began praying for Stephanie. I wrote her name in my Bible and made a point to pray for her nearly every day. I know that many others, including her husband and some close friends, were praying for her as well.

The New Testament teaches that people without Christ, like Stephanie, have a spiritual condition that is more serious than most of us realize. Their souls aren't just asleep before God; they're dead. Ephesians 2:1 says that all of us in our pre-Christ existence were dead in our sins. That's true for all people currently living without Christ. They have existence—they eat, breathe, sleep, work, feel, and procreate—but they're not living eternally. They are not enjoying a relationship with God, and there is no way they can experience the abundant life that Christ offers. The curse of sin and death has full control over them. The Bible's summary of their spiritual condition may not be pretty, but it's accurate: they're dead.

How do you pray for a lost person? How do you pray for someone whose soul is dead? With so much at stake, and with the eternal condition of the unbeliever on the line, shouldn't we be as strategic and biblical as possible when praying for spiritually dead people? We need to pray with absolute pinpoint accuracy and spiritual authority when seeking salvation for another person.

Lessons from a Tomb

Since unbelieving people are spiritually dead, perhaps we could learn from Jesus's dealings with people who were physically dead. That sounds a bit strange, but Jesus seemed to be dealing with dead people all the time. And when he finished his work with them, they were alive. In John 11, we find the exhilarating account of Jesus raising Lazarus from the dead. By studying what John writes, we can learn much about how Jesus felt about death and how he chose to deal with it. In doing so, we can learn how to pray for those held captive by spiritual death.

First, never stop praying. There is no person beyond God's reach or care. People may seem like they're unreachable, and from the human standpoint, they may be. But from God's eternal view of things, if they're still drawing breath, they can be saved. No matter what happens, never stop praying.

According to John 11, Jesus heard of Lazarus's illness with plenty of time still left for him to go to Bethany and heal Lazarus. But Jesus knew God had other things in mind, and he knew what God intended to do. Instead of rushing off to heal Lazarus, Jesus "stayed where he was two more days" (John 11:6). That must have been difficult for Jesus. He knew his friend Lazarus was suffering. He also knew that Mary and Martha wouldn't understand why he had delayed. Christ's heart must have been breaking during those long forty-eight hours. But he knew that even after Lazarus was dead, he wasn't beyond God's reach.

When Jesus finally arrived in Bethany, Lazarus had been dead for four days. That was a critical time period for Jewish people. They believed the body's decaying didn't begin until the fourth day after death. If a soul could be miraculously restored from death, it had to happen in the first three days. But after day four, when decay had set in, there was no chance of resuscitation. A soul could not be returned to a decaying body.

Mary and Martha, being good Jews, knew that when the sun rose on the fourth day after their brother's death, all hope for Jesus's raising him was gone. While Jesus's presence with them was a comfort, there really wasn't much he could do. He was too late. Lazarus was gone.

Have you ever felt that way about a person? Have you ever felt that someone you loved and cared for was beyond Jesus's reach? I certainly have.

I pray every day for all sorts of unbelieving people. Some of them seem too far gone. From all appearances, they have absolutely no interest in spiritual matters. Some of those I pray for are atheists and agnostics. Their hardwiring seems to have rendered them completely incapable of believing in God. The more I pray for them, the more their hostility toward the gospel seems to increase. Others are successful businesspeople. Their material and financial successes have dulled them to their real needs. When I pray for them, they seem to get richer and to move farther from God. Still others are very spiritual, but their spirituality translates into some form of New Age, "you are god" myth that makes them totally uninterested in Jesus.

In many cases, I get discouraged and am tempted to stop praying for these people. I'm tempted to believe that like Jesus at Lazarus's tomb, I'm too late. That's when the Spirit reminds me that no one is ever too far gone for Jesus. He gently reminds me to never stop praying for the salvation of a lost soul.

It's good to know the end of the story in John 11. Jesus wasn't too late. Lazarus wasn't beyond reach. Jesus was still able to speak into the dark, cold tomb and call his dead friend back to life. The same is true on a spiritual level. Spiritually dead people may be beyond our help, but they're not beyond hope. God can still reach them, so we should never stop praying.

When I want to stop praying, I'm frequently inspired by the following story. On October 29, 1941, during some of the darkest hours for British forces in World War II, and over a month before the United States entered the war, British Prime Minister Winston Churchill spoke to the students at the Harrow School for Boys in London. In his now-famous speech, he showed the kind of unrelenting resolve required to lead a nation during wartime:

> You cannot tell from appearances how things will go. Sometimes imagination makes things out far worse than they are. . . . Surely from this period of ten months, this is the lesson: Never give in. Never give in. Never, never, never, never—in nothing, great or small, large or petty— never give in, except to convictions of honor and good sense. Never yield to force. Never yield to the apparently overwhelming might of the enemy.[2]

I can't think of more appropriate or encouraging words for those of us engaged in the arduous work of intercession for lost souls. When you're praying for someone who is not currently interested in Christ, it's easy to draw the wrong conclusions from appearances. You pray and pray and pray, yet no real effect seems evident in the life of the person for whom you're praying. In fact, he or she may

> Your very next prayer may be the one that turns the tide and moves your lost friend toward God.

seem to be moving even farther away from God. Do not get discouraged, and do not stop praying! Remind yourself of the biblical promises about prayer and about God's desire for all people to be saved. Believe in faith that God is working, even though you can't see the results. There may be months and even years of below-the-surface work by the Holy Spirit before you ever see any evidence of it in the life of a lost person. But be fully assured: God is working.

Take Churchill's message to heart. Never give up! Never stop believing and hoping in the redemptive work of God. Your very next prayer may be the one that turns the tide and moves your lost friend toward God. Never stop praying, because it's never too late.

Second, pray that Jesus will have compassion on your lost friends. Jesus is pictured repeatedly in the Scriptures as a man of compassion. Only toward religious hypocrites did he ever show his wrath. When Jesus encountered a demoniac, a prostitute, a tax collector, or even a Pharisee with a genuine need or interest in what he had to offer, his heart seemed to break for them. Matthew reflected on Jesus's compassion when he wrote, "When he [Jesus] saw the crowds, he had compassion on them, because they were harassed and helpless, like sheep without a shepherd" (Matt. 9:36). When you're praying for a lost person to be saved, you are praying for someone who truly is a sheep without a shepherd. You can pray confidently for Jesus to deal compassionately with him or her, because he's already proven in his Word that he will.

When Jesus arrived at Mary and Martha's house, he quickly revealed his true heart toward the situation. It didn't take long for Jesus's emotions to surface when he was confronted by all the pain there. His good friends Mary and Martha were grieving. His friend Lazarus had suffered and died. Many of their friends had gathered to share in their grief. John summed it up well when he wrote, "When Jesus saw her [Mary] weeping, and the Jews who had come along with her also weeping, he was deeply moved in spirit and troubled. . . . Jesus wept" (John 11:33, 35).

What a profound scene. Jesus was truly grieved over the suffering of his friends. His heart broke for them. I think, however, there was more going on than just grief. Jesus was sad, but he was also repulsed. He hated death. He knew that death was never God's intention. Jesus hated the pain it brought and the chaos it wrought. Jesus was sickened by the despair he saw death bringing, not just to his friends but also to the world. He was truly disgusted by it.

When you're praying for Jesus to be moved with compassion over the plight of a lost person, you're on solid biblical ground. We know about the horrible condition of unbelievers because the Holy Spirit led the biblical writers to record his thoughts on the matter. In other words, everything we know about the spiritual state of the lost we learned from God. He knows better that anyone just what "lost" really means, and he was so concerned about it that he sent his Son to deal firsthand with the problem.

But just what is the plight of lost people? We've already seen that they are dead spiritually. Worse than physical death is the spiritual death that sin brings. Beyond that, however, there are other conditions facing unbelieving people that we need to be aware of and pray against.

- **Unbelieving people are spiritually blind.** In 2 Corinthians 4:4, the apostle Paul tells us they are unable to see the light of God's truth. He writes, "The god of this age has blinded the minds of unbelievers, so that they cannot see the light of the gospel of the glory of Christ, who is the image of God." The condition of spiritual blindness to which Paul refers is not self-imposed. Unbelieving people are not merely ignoring the light of God; they have been deliberately blinded to it by Satan. He has deceived them, covering their minds with a shroud of lies and half-truths. The reality and glory of Christ are hidden from them.

- **Unbelieving people are spiritual captives.** The frightening reality is that the same sinister source that blinded unbelieving people did so to control them. Obviously, unbelievers have no idea that they're actually being held captive by the world's most vicious tyrant. In Ephesians 2:1–2, Paul tells us that spiritually dead people walk and live according to the very courses and paths set out by the "ruler of the kingdom of the air"—Satan. He later adds in 2 Timothy 2:26 that Satan has taken unbelievers captive to do his evil will. There is no worse form of tyranny or oppression. A person's soul is the substance of who he or she is. To have it manipulated by the very author of evil is a most horrific fate, a fate that includes an eternity of condemnation.

- **Unbelieving people are already condemned.** Of all the conditions affecting an unbelieving person, this one may be the most upsetting for a Christian. According to Jesus himself, those who walk through life without him are living under God's hand of judgment. Jesus said, "Whoever believes in him [Jesus] is not condemned, but whoever does not believe stands condemned already because he has not believed in the name of God's one and only Son" (John 3:18). It's difficult to imagine any more depressing or disturbing scenario. Jesus promised to give abundant, eternal life to all who believe in him. Yet those who are currently rejecting him have already drawn the wrath of God because of their unbelief. They're living under the curses of sin and condemnation of death because no other provision for their sins exists. Without Jesus, their souls stand guilty before God, and their eternal future is bleak indeed.

As Jesus stood before Lazarus's tomb, he knew all the ugly realities of sin and death. He knew that often behind a physical death was a worse, more insidious spiritual one. He was repulsed by what he saw, but he was also moved by it. I'm sure it was just one more factor that helped Jesus set his face resolutely toward Jerusalem and the cross of death that awaited him there.

Jesus went to the cross out of obedience to his Father, but he also went out of compassion. He knew that he was the only hope for spiritually condemned people. He willingly died so that all people might have the chance to be forgiven. He died because his compassionate heart wouldn't let him do otherwise.

When you pray for lost people, speak to the compassionate heart of Jesus. Call on the loving and merciful God to move on behalf of captive people. Remind him that he desires for none to be lost. Remind him of the blood that Jesus shed for every person, including the person for whom you're praying. Ask him to act out of his tender and benevolent heart to do for unbelievers what they cannot do for themselves. Pray that he'll remove their blindness, set them free, and secure them in eternity.

Third, pray that Jesus will meet the unbelievers where they are. This is an important spiritual reality.

Lost people, unless they're seriously seeking God, rarely end up in church. Unless they lost a bet with a neighbor, made a deal with a mother-in-law, or are doing their token Easter/Christmas visitation, genuine unbelievers typically don't wander into churches. They have no reason to. If we're going to help them find the Christ they so desperately need, then we need to pray that Christ will find them, as he did Lazarus.

Lazarus was dead. He couldn't get to Jesus even if he'd wanted to. So it was incumbent upon Mary and Martha to get Jesus to their brother. When Jesus met with Mary and Martha outside their home in Bethany, he knew that he needed to see where Lazarus was buried. John recorded his simple question: "Where have you laid him?" (John 11:34). Mary was more than happy to show him. "Jesus, once more deeply moved, came to the tomb. It was a cave with a stone laid across the entrance" (v. 38). Notice that Jesus was still quite emotional when he approached Lazarus's tomb. We can only imagine that if the site of a person's physical tomb so moves Jesus, he is much more affected at the site of his or her spiritual tomb.

Without Christ, we entomb ourselves spiritually. The things unbelievers choose over Jesus become the sites of their spiritual burials—their spiritual crypts. People invest themselves in all sorts of hobbies, activities, work, recreation, relationships, and even addictions in an effort to find life; in reality, they're lying down in their spiritual graves.

Someone who is so determined to find his or her life's meaning in things outside the church isn't likely to spend much time there. So it is incumbent upon us, like Mary and Martha, to get Jesus to our lost loved ones. And the way we do that is through prayer.

Now, before we get too concerned that Jesus isn't likely to hang out in the types of places where our lost

Jesus has a way of getting around. I've seen him show up in some pretty unlikely places, all in the name of reaching a spiritually dead person.

friends and loved ones are, we need to remind ourselves where Jesus spent his time in his earthly ministry. John 5 showed Jesus at the Sheep Gate outside the temple walls. Hundreds of smelly sheep and just as many wounded, sick, and desperately needy people were there. It was clearly not the place to be in first-century Jerusalem. And yet that's where Jesus was, ministering to the most desperate in the group.

In Matthew 9, we learn that Matthew the tax collector threw a party so Jesus could meet several of his not-so-reputable friends. In Luke 19, Jesus had dinner in the home of a notorious tax collector named Zacchaeus. In John 3, Jesus greeted at night a spiritually inquisitive Pharisee who was either too embarrassed or too afraid to approach Jesus during the day. And in John 4, Jesus spoke to a woman who was a complete outcast in her town. Based on these examples of Jesus in the New Testament, we can know that we're on safe biblical ground when we ask Jesus to meet our unbelieving friends where they are.

Jesus has a way of getting around. I've seen him show up in some pretty unlikely places, all in the name of reaching a spiritually dead person. Jesus was in the hospital room of a dying woman who wanted to know if her soul could still be saved. He assured her that it could. Jesus marched alongside a young recruit during a difficult, twenty-mile march in boot camp, speaking to him about his need for a change in his spiritual condition. Jesus once met a friend of mine in his prison cell, and when he was released from prison he was a radically changed person. Another friend of mine, who is now in heaven, met Jesus on the streets of the New Orleans French Quarter during Mardi Gras.

I've seen Jesus on a chairlift high above a beautiful Colorado ski slope, and I've seen him on a cold, windy mountain ledge long before dawn. I've seen Jesus in the family consultation room of a hospital's emergency center, and I've seen him sweep through a crowd at a highly evangelistic funeral service. I've seen Jesus in a red-light district in London, and I've seen him in a nursing home in Fort Worth. I've seen Jesus in a counselor's office, an attorney's office, and a doctor's office. I've seen Jesus in a ski boat, in the bed of a pickup truck, on a church bus, in an ambulance, in coach on a long plane trip, and even in the cockpit of an experimental aircraft flying at ten thousand feet. And in every instance, in every one of these Jesus sightings, he was there because he was trying to get to someone who couldn't get to him.

When you're praying for unbelievers, there is nothing wrong with praying for them to go to church with you. That can be a great step in helping them find Christ. But why not start by asking Christ to find them? Picture your unbelieving friends in their study, in their bedroom, in their office, in the gym, or on the jogging trail. Think about them at school, at the computer, on a date, or giving a lecture. Ask Jesus to meet your friends there. Pray that he'll interrupt their plans and disrupt their day. Ask him to show up in the middle of their sin. Ask Jesus to ambush them in their thoughts and ideas. Encourage him to invade their privacy when they think they're all alone. Pray that they'll have an undeniable God encounter at a time and place they least expect. In short, ask Jesus to go to the place where they're buried spiritually and to start speaking life to them.

Fourth, pray that Jesus will call unbelievers by name. "Jesus called in a loud voice, 'Lazarus, come out!'"

(John 11:43). An old preacher joke about this verse states that the reason Jesus spoke to Lazarus by name is if he hadn't, every dead person in Bethany would have come out of the grave.

Have you ever thought about why Jesus used Lazarus's name? Addressing people by their names was typical for Jesus, and it wasn't just because he was being polite or friendly. Jesus tended to use names strategically, much like we do, to add emphasis to what he was saying. Sometimes he'd even begin a statement by using the person's name twice, such as "Martha, Martha" or "Simon, Simon." Now, that would get your attention.

When Jesus called Lazarus's name, he was doing several things. He showed that he knew Lazarus personally and that he was aware of his current circumstances. He knew exactly what Lazarus needed and was ready to provide it. He spoke Lazarus's name as his creator, healer, friend, and life-giver. When Jesus called Lazarus by name, he showed that he had authority over everything that was currently holding Lazarus captive.

When Jesus addresses people by name, he shows them the same things. He knows everything about them. That's why we need to pray that Jesus will speak into the heart of our unbelieving friends and loved ones and call them by name.

Let me give you another example. In the early days of the church I serve, the staff didn't have the capacity to produce any in-house videos. Whenever we needed to do a video, we hired outside help. Once we hired a professional videographer for a major project. She was just starting her own business and needed the work. In the interview process, we discovered that she was an agnostic. She found the whole idea of God to be unnecessary. Strangely enough, we hired her anyway. Our relationship with this woman quickly budded into a friendship. We found that we truly cared for her, and she found us surprisingly, well . . . cool. She'd never thought that a church group would ever need her services.

As the weeks passed, our team began to pray fervently for our new agnostic friend. We asked God to come crashing into her closed-off, private world. We asked him to ambush her and to show her his awesome glory. And we asked him to meet her where she was and to call her by name.

Since the video job required footage of our services and interviews with several of our church members, the videographer had to attend our church service a few times. That's one way to get an unbeliever to church—pay her!

On one particular Sunday, after a powerful service, our agnostic videographer walked up to me with tears in her eyes. She could barely speak. She grabbed my arm, pulled me close to her, and said something I'll never forget: "I don't believe in your God, but I felt him here today."

That's what happens when God calls someone by name. He breaks through all the pride, confusion, and excuses. When God speaks a person's name, he does so as creator, provider, healer, friend, teacher, shepherd, counselor, and lover of his or her soul. There may be no more powerful, life-altering moment for an unbeliever than when the Holy Spirit looks into the dark tomb of his or her life and quietly whispers his or her name. The Bible promises that such wooings by God—while they can be declined—cannot be ignored.

Are you praying for unbelievers? Ask God to call them by name. Pray that he will reveal himself to them as the God of the universe who knows them and loves them. He knows where they are and what they need, and he is the only one who can provide it. When you speak an unbeliever's name in prayer, pray that Jesus will speak it too.

Finally, pray that Jesus will remove what binds the unbelievers. There's a very descriptive biblical term for people without Christ: *captives*. All people traveling through life without a relationship with God are captives to Satan. As I mentioned before, Satan owns their souls, pulls their spiritual strings, and manipulates them for his evil purposes. If we're going to be serious intercessors for unbelieving people, then we have to learn to pray for Jesus to set the captives free.

Let's think once more about that amazing scene at Lazarus's tomb. Mary and Martha guided Jesus to their brother's burial site. Jesus instructed those around it to remove the stone. Jesus prayed and then called Lazarus by name. John recalled for us with amazing brevity what happened next: "The dead man came out, his hands and feet wrapped with strips of linen, and a cloth around his face" (John 11:44). It must have been a breathtaking moment. At Jesus's command, Lazarus appeared at the door to his tomb, still bound by his burial wrappings. His body had been properly prepared for burial by his grieving sisters and was probably wrapped head to toe in mummylike cloths. Upon seeing Lazarus at the tomb's entrance, Jesus issued one final command: "Take off the grave clothes and let him go" (v. 44).

Try to imagine those next few moments as people rushed to Lazarus and began removing his grave clothes. Imagine the confusion he must have felt. Think about Mary and Martha, now giddy with joy, trying through tears and laughter to explain to Lazarus what had just happened. Picture men, women, and children running through the streets of Bethany, calling to their friends and neighbors to come see this funeral in reverse. And imagine Lazarus, when his face, hands, and feet were finally free from the death restraints, embracing Jesus and thanking him for what he had done.

That, fellow Christian, is exactly what we're praying for when we ask God to liberate a captive soul.

> We need to plead with Jesus to demand that Satan free those whom he has blinded and is holding captive.

Isaiah 61:1 promised that the Messiah would be anointed to preach good news to the poor, to bind up the brokenhearted, to proclaim freedom to captives, and to release prisoners from darkness. Seven hundred years after Isaiah wrote those words, Jesus quoted them in the synagogue in Nazareth (see Luke 4:16–21). Basically, he said, "When Isaiah wrote this, he was talking about me. God's Spirit has anointed me to bring hope and healing to this land. I'm here to encourage the poor and comfort the hurting. I'm here to liberate those who have been living in bondage. Basically, I'm the deliverer you've been praying for since Isaiah wrote those words. Today your prayers are answered."

When I pray for unbelievers, I frequently remind the Lord what he said about his own mission. He came to undo what Satan had done. He came to free what Satan had bound. When people live without God, they are walking spiritual mummies. Physically they are alive, but their spiritual life and vitality has been snuffed out by sin and Satan. They are his captives, and only Jesus has the spiritual authority to set them free.

Isaiah 49 offers an encouraging promise to those who pray for spiritual captives:

> This is what the LORD says: "In the time of my favor I will answer you, and in the day of salvation I will help you . . . to say to the captives, 'Come out,' and to those in darkness, 'Be free!'"
>
> vv. 8–9

That's exactly what Jesus did at Lazarus's grave. He looked at a man held captive in the darkness of his own tomb and simply said, "Come out!" That's what we want Jesus to do for our unbelieving friends and loved ones—to speak into the darkness of their spiritual sepulchers. We want him to rebuke the lies, addictions, selfish motives, pride, fears, materialism, empty religion, false belief systems, and spiritual baggage that make up their grave clothes. More importantly, we want Jesus to rebuke the master of all spiritual darkness. We need to plead with Jesus to demand that Satan free those whom he has blinded and is holding captive. And when the dead man comes to life and is standing at his tomb's door, be ready to help him shed his grave clothes.

Conclusion

Are you ready to start pinpoint praying for unbelievers? Remember what we've learned from the example of Jesus at Lazarus's tomb.

- Never stop praying.
- Pray that Jesus will have compassion on your lost friends.
- Pray that Jesus will meet the unbelievers where they are.
- Pray that Jesus will call them by name.
- Pray that Jesus will remove what binds them.

Remember Stephanie? I opened this chapter talking about her struggles with spiritual skepticism. Before she was baptized in a lake outside of Austin, she stood before a large crowd, surrounded by friends and family, and thanked those who had helped her cross the line and embrace Jesus. It was an emotional statement for her. It was emotional for all of us who had been praying for her. She is living proof of the reality that Jesus still sets captives free and that he still gives life to the spiritually dead.

At the end of Stephanie's testimony, she shared, "I have felt the Holy Spirit inside me, guiding me, and now I am ready to be a servant." Five months after her baptism, Stephanie chose to spend Thanksgiving weekend in Juarez, Mexico, feeding poor and displaced people with a group from our church. She took along a friend who was going through a tough time so she could minister to her. She has also joined a women's Bible study. Stephanie tried to let me down gently when she told me she would no longer be attending my skeptics class. I guess she figured it was finally time for her to graduate.

Never stop praying. Jesus is in the business of setting captives free, of breathing life into the spiritually dead, and of turning skeptics into servants.

Discussion Questions

1. This chapter opened with the story of Stephanie, a woman who was very far from God. Do you have any Stephanies in your life for whom you are currently praying? Describe one.
2. When you pray for these people, what do you say to God?
3. Have you ever been tempted to stop praying for a lost friend? Have you given up and stopped praying for someone who seemed too far from God or who was taking too long to become a Christian? Where is that person now?
4. Think of a person whom you want to become a Christian. Which one of the pinpoint prayers in this

chapter (*Jesus, have compassion on them*; *Jesus, meet them where they are*; *Jesus, call them by name*; *Jesus, set them free*) do you think might be the most effective for him or her? Why?

5. After reading this chapter, how do you think God feels about your unbelieving friends and family? How will you pray differently for them?

5

HELP!

Pinpoint Praying in Crisis Times

Now, Lord, consider their threats and enable your servants to speak your word with great boldness.

Acts 4:29

I t wasn't one of my more graceful moments. Fourteen-year-old boys tend to be all ears, elbows, and feet, and I was certainly no exception. But my current predicament seemed only to compound my awkwardness. I was literally between a rock and a hard place.

I was at about 14,100 feet above sea level, on one of the tallest and toughest climbs in Colorado, especially for a fourteen-year-old novice. I was climbing with my father and my two older sisters on the final ascent to the mountain's summit. The mountain's face was steep and potentially very dangerous. I had been making my way up a six-inch-wide crack, using it for both hand- and footholds. The crack had petered out, so I was trying to transition to another crack about three feet away. I reached over with my right hand and foot and almost caught a hold in the crack—*almost*. My lanky limbs were able to reach only to the edge of the crack. Before I could pull them back and resecure myself in my present hold, my left foot and hand slipped, and I fell against the face of the mountain.

There I was, straddling two points on a mountain wall, with all of my weight now pressed against the mountain. Veteran climbers know that the minute you forfeit your four-point stance of only hands and feet touching the mountain, you're in big trouble. That was me. I was wearing a backpack, and I could feel the relentless claws of gravity grasping at it, trying desperately to pull me over backward. I felt that if I even took a deep breath, the extra air in my lungs would be enough to topple me over and send me careening down the mountain wall. Like I said, it wasn't one of my more graceful moments.

So I whispered, "Help." Even using an exclamation point at the end of that word would imply more force than there was in my cry. I just barely whispered the word, and it was so quiet *I* almost didn't hear it. But that was all the effort I could afford. Anything more dramatic might have cost me my perch. But the moment the word was off my lips, I felt a huge hand slipping under my stomach and around my waist. Suddenly I was being pulled over onto the new and more secure crack. Once I was stable, I looked up into the face of my rescuer—my dad. He just shook his head, muttered something like, "Clumsy," and then turned and continued up the mountain. (Mercy doesn't run particularly deep in my family.) I took a big, deep breath and then let out a full and relieved sigh. I thought I might just live to see another day. Somehow my feeble cry for help had been heard. I had been rescued.

Have you ever been so much between a rock and a hard place that it was all you could do to muster a weak prayer for help? Have you ever felt so cornered in life that you didn't know how you could survive another day? How do you respond when a real crisis kicks in? How do you pray?

Pinpoint praying is not just for making big asks of God or for seeking salvation for a friend. Pinpoint praying can also make a major difference when walking through crisis. In fact, effective pinpoint praying can be what makes the difference between just enduring and prevailing through a difficult time.

Crisis: A Really Great Time to Panic

Consider the Old Testament example of Daniel. He has to be one of the best role models in the Bible for effective pinpoint praying in crisis times. Just about all of Daniel's life could be summed up by the word *crisis*.

Daniel was probably an orphan, and he was living in a foreign land as part of a captive people. Most of his countrymen had been slaughtered by the Babylonian King Nebuchadnezzar's army. A few select young men had been spared and taken back to Babylon for "reformatting" into Babylonian ways. Daniel and three of his friends were some of those young men.

Daniel and his friends determined to remain faithful to God's law, even though they were six hundred miles from home, they were in a pagan land that worshiped pagan gods, and their nation no longer existed. God honored their faithfulness, and Daniel and his friends were quickly elevated to leadership roles within the kingdom.

They were recognized as part of the group of seers and prophets that the king kept nearby.

On one particular day, the king had a terrible nightmare and wanted to know what his dream meant. He called in some of his seers and asked them to interpret his dream (see Dan. 2:1–13). I really would have liked to be a fly on the wall for that conversation, which went something like this:

Seers: Long live the king! How can we serve you?

King: I have endured terrible suffering because of a dream I had. I want you to tell me what it means.

Seers: O great king, we are sorry for your suffering. But we are just what you need. We can certainly interpret your dream and relieve your suffering.

King (after a long pause): Go ahead then. Tell me.

Seers: Uh, excuse us, O great and mighty one, but we need you to tell us the dream. Then we can certainly interpret it for you.

King: No.

Seers: No?

King: No.

Seers: Uh, please excuse us again, O king, but if you do not tell us the dream, we can't interpret it.

King: Of course you can! For all that I pay you, you guys should be able to do this in your sleep! Any seer worth his salt can both tell a dream and then interpret it. How else do I know if you guys are the real deal? You could just make up some crazy tale and say that it's what my dream means. No way. If I'm going to believe you, then you've got to both tell me the dream *and* interpret it.

Seers: O king, we know that you are both great and wise, but there is not a man alive who can know the dreams of another. What you ask of us is impossible.

King: Then you will all die—you and all the other worthless seers and prophets. I'll kill every last one of you. What good is a group of prophets who can't even tell me my dream? You've got twenty-four hours to figure it out.

That, my friends, is a real crisis. Suddenly Daniel and his friends were facing death for something that had nothing to do with them. Had God spared them in Jerusalem just so they could be brought to Babylon and executed? Could things have been any worse for Daniel? He and his friends were less than a day away from a date with a Babylonian sword, and as far as they were concerned, they were powerless to do anything about it.

What's your crisis? Is it your health, your finances, or your employment? Is it a relationship or a long bout with depression? Is it an addiction you can't seem to overcome? Do you have an unwed child who is pregnant or a parent with Alzheimer's? Our church is filled with people who are facing long-term unemployment, the imminent loss of a loved one, or the end of a marriage. Every day we have people whose businesses fail or whose sons or daughters are shipped off to war. There are those facing lawsuits and those with severely handicapped children. Some are grieving a miscarriage, while others grieve missed opportunities. In short, there is crisis all around. There always will be.

The question we face as Christ-followers is not how to avoid crisis, because we can't. The question is whether or not we know how to respond when it comes calling. More specifically, do we know how to pray when crisis

Help!

breaks out in our lives? In the world we live in today, that may well be the question of the hour.

I'd like to offer a working definition of *crisis*: "when life suddenly increases in pace, pressure, and problems with no immediate resolution or relief in sight." Did you notice the two ingredients in a crisis? First, there's increased stress—increased pace, pressure, and problems—which can lead to increased pain. Second, there's the ongoing nature of the crisis. Either you don't see an end to the painful circumstances or you don't see a viable way out.

The only option for Daniel and his friends seemed to be death. That's a crisis—increased emotional and even physical discomfort with no apparent relief on the horizon. The very best solution to crisis times is pinpoint praying. Daniel is a great example of how we should respond in prayer when the bombs start falling all around us.

Peacetime Praying

One of the most important factors in crisis pinpoint praying is to be a person of prayer *before* the crisis hits. A crisis is not the time to *start* praying; it's the time to *keep* praying. That isn't always easy. It's typically a crisis that drives us to prayer. When things are just rocking along, we usually don't feel the need to pray. But we need to pray "in season and out" (2 Tim. 4:2), in good times and bad. Be a praying person before the hurricane blows through your life, and then when it does, you won't have to try to start praying.

Consider Daniel. We know that he was a highly commit-

> A crisis is not the time to *start* praying; it's the time to *keep* praying.

ted man of prayer. He didn't pray just when he was in trouble. He chose to pray daily—several times a day, in fact—regardless of his circumstances. Daniel chose to keep praying even when prayer had been outlawed in Babylon: "Three times a day he got down on his knees and prayed, giving thanks to his God, just as he had done before" (Dan. 6:10). Did you catch that last part? "Just as he had done before." Prayer wasn't new for Daniel. It was standard operating procedure. When the crisis came, all he had to do was *keep* praying.

Is prayer part of your daily routine, or is it reserved just for those seasons of trial? Let me provide some reasons to keep up what I call "peacetime praying."

- **Peacetime praying builds spiritual momentum.** Prayer brings God's blessing and God's provision. A praying person lives with the kind of spiritual momentum and favor that only consistent prayer can bring. You want to be fully armed and ready with all the spiritual gumption God can provide when the crisis hits. Peacetime praying helps equip and prepare you for the crisis times sure to come.

- **Peacetime praying produces spiritual intimacy.** Prayer brings you closer to God, and you'll need all the intimacy with God you can get when the storms break out. I'm sure this is partly why Paul encouraged us to "pray without ceasing" (1 Thess. 5:17 NASB). He knew firsthand the importance of storing up spiritual intimacy for those difficult times of suffering that would drain him dry. Paul, like Daniel, kept his intimacy with God intact throughout his trials because he was close to God *before* the trouble came. Peacetime praying helps you build the intimacy with God you'll need to weather your storms.

- **Peacetime praying provides spiritual perspective.** When you're in a crisis, get ready for the mind games that Satan will no doubt try to play on you. Remember, all he can do is lie, and he just loves doing so to Christians in crisis. Consider these lies: *If you had been a better Christian, this never would have happened. You deserve all the pain you're feeling. It's about time you start paying for your sins. God's obviously forgotten about you. Nobody he loves would ever suffer like this. What good has your faith done you? You've tried to be a good Christian, and look what it's gotten you—sorrow and suffering.*

Have you ever heard any of these lies? I certainly have. And if I don't have a healthy dose of spiritual perspective, I just might start believing them. Peacetime praying girds my heart and mind with the spiritual truths I will need to make it through tough times. It builds a strong defense against the lies Satan will hurl my way. If I'm not practicing prayer in good seasons, then I'm a sitting duck for satanic attack when the pain really kicks in.

Right now, determine to be a peacetime pray-er so that you can be prepared for your next crisis. Apply Daniel's example of disciplined prayer to your life and be a steady man or woman of prayer before you have to dial 911. Here are a few suggestions:

- **Have a regular prayer time.** Don't wonder when or if you'll get to pray again. Have a set time for prayer and ruthlessly protect it. Be as committed to prayer as you are to meals.
- **Have a regular prayer place.** Don't wonder where you'll be able to find a quiet place for prayer. Build a location into your discipline of peacetime praying. When your set time for prayer rolls around, be unyielding about staying in your set place.

- **Have a regular prayer plan.** Don't wonder what you'll say to God when you pray. Be systematic about your conversations with him. I use my Bible as my daily prayer guide. I can open it on any day and have plenty to talk to God about. Should the Spirit choose to lead me to different subjects, I try to be sensitive and obedient to that. But when I sit down to talk with God, I know where I intend to go. It takes much of the guesswork and wasted time out of my precious moments with God.

As sure as you're reading these words, your next crisis is already brewing. It may be months before it blows, but it will. At that time, you don't want to make confessing your prayerlessness part of your crisis praying. You don't want to wonder if the crisis is the result of your lack of prayer. And you don't want to have to overcome distance with God because you haven't been spending time with him. None of these things is a good option in crisis time. So be a Daniel. Be praying in advance of the attack. That way, when the fire does break out in your life, you'll be prepared to keep right on praying.

Will You Pray for Me?

One of the first things Daniel did when he heard of the death sentence was to rally his fellow pray-ers:

> Then Daniel returned to his house and explained the matter to his friends. . . . He urged them to plead for mercy from the God of heaven concerning this mystery, so that he and his friends might not be executed with the rest of the wise men of Babylon.
>
> Daniel 2:17–18

This was no time for a solo act. Daniel knew that he needed all the prayer support he could get if he and his friends were to survive this crisis. He also knew there was comfort to be found in praying with others. The following story helped me understand just how important prayer is in crisis times.

A few years ago, some elementary-age boys got lost in a cave not far from where I live. They were missing for only a few hours, but the time was more than enough to terrify them and their parents and to call out nearly every emergency worker in the Austin area. The boys were rescued unharmed, and the story was front-page news the next day. One of the older boys, Brandon, told a reporter about their time in the cave: "We prayed twenty times out loud, and then some of us slept. Bobby even snored. We prayed that if we ever got out of there, we would never go in again."

Isn't that a wonderful picture of the companionship of prayer? First, you pray like crazy. You pray, you make pledges to God, and then you sleep. There's something really comforting about knowing that not only are other people walking through the crisis with you, but they're also praying with you for God's miraculous provision.

When Daniel realized that he and his friends were in big trouble, he circled the prayer wagons. He had the sense to know that not only was there great power in corporate prayer, but there was also great comfort in it.

Are you humble and wise enough to seek the prayers of others when your crises come? Culture has preconditioned us to act strong and fly solo in tough times. Asking for help, especially prayer, can be a sign of real weakness. But guess what? You are weak. The types of trials that Satan creates and God allows are not the kind you can survive alone. You're not showing weakness when you seek prayer in times of trouble; you're showing wisdom. The holy Son of God didn't try to face his crises without the prayers of others; neither should you.

A Prayer I'll Never Forget

On March 2, 1997, my mother almost died. She had never been really healthy, at least not that I could remember. But even all her years of relative unhealthiness didn't prepare us for that day. It was a Sunday, and I had just finished preaching at our second service. Someone found me and told me that I had an emergency phone call. It was my father, who was at the emergency room with my mom, and he thought she was having a heart attack. Actually, a heart attack would have been good news.

My mother had a urinary tract infection that had become septic. In other words, the infection had spread to her bloodstream and was poisoning her body. When septicemia hits a person, total physiological chaos breaks out. It's like having a vicious poison injected directly into the bloodstream. Over the next several hours, just about every major organ in my mother's body shut down. She eventually did suffer complete cardiac arrest—after her liver, kidneys, and lungs ceased to function. Her heart attack was followed by a stroke. She was in her midsixties, and because of her already poor health, we were told not just to prepare for the worst but to expect it.

It's amazing how a family that is typically polished and put together can feel so inadequate and out of place in a hospital waiting room. We were all so used to being strong and self-assured. As a pastor, I was used to caregiving, but as I huddled with my family in the ICU waiting area, I couldn't offer care to anyone. We all felt completely overwhelmed. We were no longer the strong, sophisticated, rock-solid family we thought we were.

Help!

89

None of us knew what to do or say. We just sat there in numb silence. And then *my* pastor showed up.

He had been retired for several years. His own bout with a medical crisis had cut short a thriving ministry. I had been raised under his teaching and had been saved, baptized, called, ordained, and married under his skillful leadership. He was and always will be my pastor. It didn't take him long to surmise that we were a collective mess and that we needed some serious support. After a few brief words of comfort, he asked a question that changed the tenor of the entire evening: "Can we pray?"

Between my immediate family, extended family, and friends, there were easily thirty of us in the group. We took up a large section of the waiting room, where others had also gathered to support each other and keep vigil for their critically ill loved ones. My pastor instructed us to form a circle and join hands; so we did, right there in the middle of a downtown Austin hospital, and then my pastor prayed. I really don't remember anything he said. But I remember his voice—calm, confident, and comforting—and I remember his strength. The man prayed as if he knew the crisis wouldn't win the day. He prayed as if he knew that the very Creator of the universe would personally guide us through the perilous next few hours and days. He prayed like he'd prayed a thousand other crisis pinpoint prayers before.

When he finished, I looked around at our group. We were all crying. I knew then that no matter what happened, whether my mom lived or died, we would get through the crisis. Strength had come, comfort had been extended, hope had been gained—and it had all happened in prayer.

That's what the fellowship of prayer does. It offers perspective in a crisis that would otherwise appear to be insurmountable. Daniel sought fellowship in prayer. So did Paul, the early church leaders, and Jesus. In each case, the comfort of shared prayers gave them the strength to keep moving through the crisis.

What about you? Are the bombs falling yet? If so, rally your praying friends. If not, put your friends on notice, because at some point in the not-so-distant future, you're going to need each other.

Big-Picture Praying

There is one more aspect to pinpoint praying in crisis times, and it's probably the most important one. Ultimately, it involves making some very specific requests of God. In many of the trials we face, we know exactly what is needed to either make the problem disappear or at least help us bear up under it. It may be miraculous healing, financial provision, a broken and contrite heart for a person in sin, clear direction in a pressing decision, relational restoration, or rescue from danger. And in these cases, that's exactly what we should ask for. The crisis reveals the need, and we pray for it.

In other crises, however, we'll sense that God wants not to deliver us from the crisis but to guide us through it. On September 11, 2001, when we sat by our television sets and watched in horror as the two towers of the World Trade Center collapsed into rubble, we knew that there would be no quick deliverance from this national crisis. It was time to pray for strength to prevail through it. In either case—deliverance or perseverance—you need to know what you want God to do and have the spiritual gumption to ask him specifically for it.

That's precisely what Daniel did. He rallied his friends and urged them to "plead for mercy from the God of heaven concerning this mystery" (Dan. 2:18). They asked God to show them something they would never discover otherwise. Later, after God had spoken to him, Daniel

Help!

thanked God for giving him wisdom and power and for making known to him what he asked for—the king's dream (see Dan. 2:23).

Daniel and his friends faced their crisis by praying with pinpoint accuracy about what they needed. I find their courage and insight amazing. They could have asked God to strike down King Nebuchadnezzar and remove the threat altogether. They could have prayed for some kind of divine rescue from their captivity in Babylon. They even could have prayed for God to make known the dream to the seers so that they wouldn't have to die. But that's not what they settled for. Daniel and his friends chose to ask not only for the impossible but also for that which would give God the most glory. They knew that their God could indeed reveal the deepest secrets of a man's heart. They knew that if he chose to, he could easily tell them the king's dream and its meaning. And they knew that the best way for this crisis to be resolved was for God to come through with exactly what the king was seeking. Nebuchadnezzar hadn't asked for too much; he just unwittingly asked for what only God could do. That's precisely what Daniel and his friends prayed for, and they got it.

In Acts 4, after Peter and John had been threatened and commanded not to speak in Jesus's name, they prayed for the solution that would bring the most glory to God and require divine provision from him. They prayed for boldness. I love that. They asked not for deliverance from the threats but rather boldness in the face of them. Like the 9/11 events of our day, their crisis wasn't going away. They knew they had to prevail through it, so they prayed with pinpoint accuracy for courage: "Now, Lord, consider their threats

> It takes real spiritual maturity to seek God for something other than deliverance in a crisis.

and enable your servants to speak your word with great boldness" (v. 29). Like Daniel, they received the very same miraculous provision that they were looking for: "After they prayed, the place where they were meeting was shaken. And they were all filled with the Holy Spirit and spoke the word of God boldly" (v. 31).

It takes real spiritual maturity to seek God for something other than deliverance in a crisis. Crisis pinpoint praying doesn't always involve praying for and receiving rescue. It requires maturity enough to seek the heart and will of God. It requires us to long for his holy name to be glorified, even in the midst of terrible crisis. Had God simply made Daniel's crisis disappear, the chance for God to be exalted before the eyes of a pagan king would have been missed. Instead, Daniel prayed for a miracle that had much more personal risk for him—and God came through.

> King Nebuchadnezzar fell prostrate before Daniel and paid him honor and ordered that an offering and incense be presented to him. The king said to Daniel, "Surely your God is the God of gods and the Lord of kings and a revealer of mysteries, for you were able to reveal this mystery."
>
> Daniel 2:46–47

The risk paid off. Not only did God come through for Daniel, but he exalted his own name in the process.

How many times have you missed God's pinpoint provision in a crisis because you prayed for the easiest way out? If you believe that God is sovereign, then every circumstance of your life—including crisis—is under his control. You know that God can eliminate a crisis or problem instantaneously; if he hasn't chosen to, then you need to be looking for more than just deliverance from it. Questions like "God, what are you trying to accomplish?" or "God, what are you wanting to do in me through this crisis?" or "God, how can your name be glorified here?" become supremely relevant.

Crisis pinpoint praying involves discerning all that is at stake besides your comfort. It will often mean that you have to pray for grace to prevail through the storm rather than be rescued from it. Daniel didn't pray for the crisis to go away; he prayed for God to do something miraculous through it. That is a pinpoint prayer God will answer. Set aside your desire for personal protection and fling yourself out before God as a vessel to be used even in crisis, and you'll find God exalting himself in every aspect of your life.

That, by the way, is exactly what Jesus did. When he was facing the cross, he made a very specific pinpoint request of God for deliverance. He asked his Father to take the cup of the cross away from him. But coupled with his prayer for deliverance was a prayer of submission. He openly acknowledged his willingness to walk the path that would be consistent with God's will and bring the most glory to his name. Like Daniel, Jesus prayed for an end to the crisis that would exalt God the most.

We know the end of the story: Jesus had to walk through the crisis in order to accomplish God's will and plan. His pinpoint prayer for God's highest glory was answered with God's pinpoint provision that enabled him to walk a path of human suffering unmatched in history. And it was Jesus's difficult but obedient walk to the cross that brought the most honor to God's name.

What crisis are you facing right now? What specific thing do you want God to do in it? Boldly ask him for it. But in your prayer, have the maturity to submit to the work of God that you can't see. While you're praying for a tumor to be removed, pray for God to be exalted in the faith and life of that patient. While you're praying for a conflict to be resolved, pray that God will be honored in how the conflict is handled. While you're praying for financial provision, ask God to be glorified in your faith when the provision is slow in coming.

Here's the bottom line on crisis pinpoint praying: pray for the specific deliverance you seek, but along with that, ask God to resolve the crisis in a way that honors him and allows for the greatest display of his power, love, and mercy. Yield to his ways, even if it means that your deliverance is delayed. Pray for God to make himself famous in your crisis. That is crisis pinpoint praying that God answers.

"I Want to Glorify God"

I recently attended a two-day prayer retreat with about fifty other pastors. One of them had lost his twenty-seven-year-old son just six weeks before. He was killed in a tragic accident while attending a one-day training seminar in Chicago. This pastor's wounds were still raw. He thanked the men in the room whose churches had supported him during his family's nightmare, but he still couldn't speak about his loss without tears. I ended up in a small group with him talking about—ironically enough—the hard side of ministry.

This man is living in crisis. Ever since a policeman knocked on his door at 5:00 in the morning six weeks before, all he has known is a blur of pain and profound sadness. Every day he wakes up with the pain of knowing that he'll never see his son again. He commented that even drawing the next breath is a challenge, and he wouldn't have the strength to except for the prayers of God's people.

This pastor and his family are walking through a crisis from which there is no quick deliverance. There will be no dramatic prison breaks or closing of lions' mouths.

No midnight revelations will help this family get their son back. Their crisis pinpoint prayers are, at this point, all about survival.

But even in his pain, the pastor had perspective. "I want to glorify God," he said. "I want to be able to look back on this and see the ways that God exalted himself through my son's death." And that's what we prayed for. We asked God to show himself strong for this family in crisis. We prayed that he would be their comforter and healer. We asked God to greet their son in heaven on their behalf. And we asked God to give them strength to walk out this difficult assignment he had given them. There were no pinpoint prayers for deliverance, just ones for strength.

When you seek to honor God in your crisis no matter what the cost, you will. God will make sure that you do.

By the way, my mother survived her initial brush with death. After two years in and out of the hospital and even a six-month engagement with hospice waiting for her to die, my mom simply got stronger. At the time of this writing, nearly a decade after she became so ill, she's alive, robust, and quick-witted, and she has an opinion about everything. Yea, God. Pinpoint praying works.

Discussion Questions

1. What has been the most difficult crisis you have faced personally in the last year? How did you deal with it? What role did prayer play in the process?
2. How spiritually prepared do you feel today if a crisis were to come? What are your current patterns of peacetime praying?
3. Do you have people in your life who you know pray regularly for you? Why or why not? If a crisis hit

today, how many people could you call or email to request prayer?

4. Can you think of a time when you might have cut short God's work in a crisis simply because you sought the quick route to deliverance? How do you feel about praying for God's will and honor—not necessarily your deliverance—in the midst of a crisis?

5. In light of this chapter, how will your prayers and behaviors in crises change?

Help!

6

LORD, WE AGREE
Pinpoint Praying with Other Christians

Again, I tell you that if two of you on earth agree about anything you ask for, it will be done for you by my Father in heaven.

Matthew 18:19

I remember it like it was yesterday. I was in a church staff meeting on a Tuesday morning. Our church secretary walked in and quickly apologized for interrupting the meeting. We could tell that it was urgent. She had crunched our financial numbers and realized that we didn't have enough money in the bank to make it through the week.

Those were the early, trying days of our church. It was a season of our church's life where every penny counted. We were a small organization with only a few staff and a very small budget. We literally lived from week to week, from offering to offering. We had been in tight spots before, but never *this* tight. Now we had bills due and not nearly enough money to cover them all. If something

didn't happen, we'd be delin-
quent with several creditors.
For a church trying to reach
unchurched people and establish a name in a city, that's the
unpardonable sin.

If you're looking for
pinpoint prayers that
have off-the-charts
potential, then learn
to pray with other
Christians.

We considered our options.
The most obvious was to send
up a major smoke signal for
help. We could get on the
phone, send out emails, and beg people to step up and
give. But even with that plan, we had no guarantees that
we'd receive the revenues in time. We also ran the risk
of alienating some new Christians and new members by
making such a desperate plea.

After discussing it, I proposed a different course of
action. I told the staff that we were going to pray right
then as a team and also meet each morning for prayer for
the rest of the week. We decided to tell no one else about
our need—no one, that is, except God. We committed
to pray together—to agree in our hearts to ask for God's
provision and wait for him to come through.

So we prayed that morning and every day that week.
What happened next now resides in the file of "great
moments in our church's history." Money started pour-
ing in—not in huge amounts but in small yet numer-
ous doses. People who had never given before suddenly
felt led to drop by and write a check. Others called and
wanted to transfer stock. It happened that way every
day. By the week's end, we had paid every bill and had a
reasonable cushion to build on for the rest of the month.
And in all that time, we never told anyone of our need;
we just prayed together.

Today when we're in tight spots as a church or trying to make huge faith-based decisions, we always remember that strategic week. We learned not just that

Pray Big

God provides but also that he honors corporate prayer. We learned that there is something amazingly powerful about Christians praying together.

Holy Ground

Jesus was an advocate of corporate prayer. He believed in it, practiced it, and taught it. In fact, it's difficult to overstate the significance Christ placed on it. If you're looking for pinpoint prayers that have off-the-charts potential, then learn to pray with other Christians.

Why is the prayer meeting (for those churches that still have them) the least attended meeting in the church? Why are prayer ministries struggling to find volunteers? Why have most men yielded the role of intercession to women? Why are so few Christians comfortable praying out loud with other Christians? Why don't pastors and other spiritual leaders spend more time praying together? Why don't more husbands and wives pray together? For all of the promise and authority that Jesus gave to group intercession, it sure gets little airtime in Christians' lives today. It's almost as if there is an organized effort bent on keeping Christians from praying together. Hmm . . .

In Matthew 18:19, Jesus made a sweeping statement about the unlimited impact that corporate prayer could have in the church. He said, "Again, I tell you that if two of you on earth agree about anything you ask for, it will be done for you by my Father in heaven." This wasn't an isolated comment by Jesus. He had just finished warning about the dangers of conflict and unconfronted sin in the church. He gave specific instructions to all believers so we could avoid the kind of church blowouts for which the church has become notorious. It was like he was saying, "At all costs, protect the unity of your church."

Immediately after verse 19, Jesus tells us why corporate prayer is so powerful: "For where two or three come together in my name, there am I with them" (v. 20). In other words, "Whenever believers gather together, I'm there."

There is a powerful, mystical beauty in a simple meeting of believers. Jesus paid it the highest compliment and gave it the greatest authority possible. Jesus isn't obligated to be anywhere, but he promised that when a group meets together in his name, even if there are just two of them, he will be there with them.

As a pastor, I find that very encouraging. I don't have to lead a large congregation to merit God's presence. Elders meetings have just as much attraction to Jesus as worship services. When we as a staff seek God, when a small group meets to study the Bible, or even when I'm counseling someone in my office, God's full presence is there with us. There are no wasted gatherings in the church, as long as those who gather do so in Jesus's name.

But this sweeping promise tells me something else: a gathering of believers is more powerful than any other meeting on the planet. A group of women meeting to pray for their church's needs has more power and authority than a joint session of Congress. A men's accountability group that meets in Jesus's name has more spiritual power than the Joint Chiefs of Staff has military power. A family Bible study has more authority than a meeting of the U.S. Supreme Court.

The most powerful gatherings in the world are those that meet in Jesus's name. When they meet aligning with his purposes and seeking his glory, he is there with them.

> A gathering of believers is more powerful than any other meeting on the planet.

We Can Make Beautiful Music Together

In Matthew 18:19, Jesus used a descriptive term to help his disciples understand why praying together is so powerful. Our English Bibles typically use the word *agree*, but that doesn't do it justice. The word Jesus used is the Greek word *symphōneō*, and you can probably see its similarity to our word *symphony*. At its most basic meaning, the word means "to sound the same." Thus we get the meanings "to agree," "to be in one accord," or "to be harmonious." When Jesus used this word, he obviously had in mind the appealing sound of his people praying for the same things. And while Jesus probably wasn't thinking of a symphony, it's still a great illustration of what he meant.

When musicians unite together—each with his or her special gifts and talents, each playing a different role and instrument—to produce a beautiful musical piece, the experience can be incredibly moving and inspiring. The reverse is true as well. When each musician tries to do his or her own thing or drown out the other players, the result is disastrous. No one wants to listen to the painful noise a group of competing or out-of-sync musicians makes.

The same is true of God and prayer. He loves to hear the corporate, unified prayers of his people. That's why Jesus spoke so highly of prayer meetings. They really are music to God's ears.

Christianity is not an individual sport. God clearly laid out the path of the Christ-follower to include community and fellowship with other believers. Corporate prayer may be the most intimate expression of Christian unity. When believers set aside their personal agendas and together seek God's answers, they've broken into a new stratosphere of pinpoint prayer. Quite frankly, there may be no more effective words a Christian can say in prayer than "Lord, I agree." And when we agree, Jesus promised that God will give us what we ask.

Reasons to Agree

Do you pray with other Christians? Are you part of the symphony of intercession that makes beautiful music to the Father's ears? If you're a typical believer, your answer is no. Far too few Christ-followers see the value of or commit the time to interceding corporately. Others of us are so intimidated by praying out loud that we don't dare put ourselves in a situation where we might be asked to pray. In short, we're silencing the symphony, and our reasons for doing so are pathetic.

In light of that reality, I want to try to fire you up a bit. Since corporate pinpoint praying is an incredibly effective level of spiritual intercession, I want to motivate you to make it a major priority in your life. I want you to be so convinced of the power of praying with other Christians that you'll start recruiting others to join you in prayer. Here are some amazing biblical truths about corporate pinpoint prayer.

Great spiritual authority is given to agreeing Christians. Besides the words of Jesus in Matthew 18, we have other biblical calls for believers to intercede together. James 5:14 says, "Is any one of you sick? He should call the elders of the church to pray over him and anoint him with oil in the name of the Lord." James exhorted any ailing disciple to call the elders together for prayer. His point was that the agreement of such qualified leaders for the healing of the individual would certainly attract the attention of God.

The apostle Paul urged the believers in Ephesus to "pray in the Spirit on all occasions with all kinds of prayers and requests. With this in mind, be alert and always keep on praying for all the saints" (Eph. 6:18). He urged them to make sure their corporate gatherings were marked by significant times of prayer. Remember that it was the agreeing prayers of the believers in Acts 12 that led to Peter's miraculous escape from Herod's prison. And perhaps most dramatically, the Holy Spirit was first poured out upon the earth in the upper room where 120 had gathered to pray. In other words, the New Testament church was born in a prayer meeting.

Agreeing prayer reflects Jesus's unity with his Father. In John 17, before Jesus was arrested, he prayed at length for the unity of his followers. He prayed that his followers would be one and that they would reflect the very love and unity that existed between him and his Father. This was very important to Jesus—important enough to be on his mind in the hours before his impending death.

Jesus knew how intimacy with his Father had impacted his life and ministry. He could perform miracles and teach with authority because God heard him when he prayed, and God heard him because he and the Father were one. Jesus knew his disciples would have no real spiritual authority if they weren't a tightly knit unit. He knew a house divided against itself couldn't stand. So he prayed for his followers to have singleness of mind. He did so knowing that such unity would mirror his own oneness with his Father.

When Christians agree in prayer, they model the kind of unity and intimacy that Jesus prayed for in John 17. The result is they experience the very power and favor the Son knew in his intimacy with the Father. No wonder agreeing prayer yields kingdom fruit; it's as if Jesus himself is praying with us.

Agreeing prayer humbles those who participate. The Bible tells us that God is drawn to those with broken spirits and that the meek shall inherit the earth. It teaches that the last shall be first and that those who humble themselves will be exalted. Few things are more humbling than praying out loud in agreement with other Christians. God honors humility, and corporate prayer humbles. That is why it's so powerful.

When you pray with other Christians, you have to set aside your selfish desires and personal agenda. You have to be willing to align your heart with those around you and seek the favor of God for the whole, not just for you. It's an act of spiritual self-abasement that God acknowledges and honors. Group pinpoint praying is powerful because it makes each intercessor a teachable, pliable tool in God's hands.

Are you motivated yet? Are you ready to set aside your spiritual inhibitions and become a group pinpoint intercessor? Have the realities of how God blesses agreeing prayer moved you out of your comfort zone of prayer? There is so much to be gained by circling up with other believers and seeking God together. Why not get on the phone right now and schedule time to meet with some friends for prayer? God's power is ready to be unleashed for those who will come together and agree.

Abby's Story

June 19, 1995

Dearest Abby, you entered our lives ten days ago. It's hard to believe it's already been that long. Poor sweet baby, you have had a very rough entrance into the world. I can't tell you how helpless I feel. I want to protect you from all the pain you are experiencing in ICU, but there's not a whole lot more I can do other than be here beside you. . . . The doctors are telling us that you won't be with us for long—I can't bear the thought of life without you in it.[3]

Abby Marie Jimmerson entered the world tumultuously on June 9, 1995, a full six weeks before her due date. Besides being dangerously early and enduring a difficult delivery, Abby was quickly diagnosed with trisomy 18 syndrome, a chromosome disorder that affects one in six thousand infants. Trisomy 18 babies can have extreme birth defects, including congenital heart defects, and have a tragically high infant mortality rate. Abby appeared to be no exception. She weighed only 4.3 pounds and had a failed swallowing mechanism, a completely blocked sinus cavity, and a major heart defect. Abby was fighting for her life from the moment she drew her first breath. Her battle was one doctors did not expect her to win. Her parents, Wendy and Jim, were told to prepare for the worst.

I didn't know Wendy and Jim very well when I got the call about Abby. My brother-in-law, a good friend of theirs, called and asked if I and some of the elders could lay hands on Abby and pray for her. Not knowing what to expect, we headed to the neonatal ICU in Austin's Brackenridge Children's Hospital. It was a gut-wrenching experience. Every baby in the ICU ward had serious health issues, and little Abby was the worst.

She was just a tiny bundle of baby surrounded by wires and high-tech gadgets. She was so small that we couldn't really lay our hands on her, but we did the best we could. We circled around Abby and prayed, along with her parents, that God would spare her life.

In over twenty-five years of pastoral ministry, those few moments of pinpoint prayer for Abby are some of the most profound and moving that I've ever experienced. We all cried. Abby was so helpless and weak. We felt this overwhelming urge to protect and defend her from all the pain she was experiencing. All that emotion and desire came out in the form of passionate agreeing prayer. Right there in the middle of the neonatal ICU, with doctors and nurses hovering close by, we prayed for the God of heaven to save and heal her. We begged God to do for Abby what we could not. We prayed a big, hairy, audacious prayer on behalf of a tiny baby who couldn't pray for herself. I'll never forget that time.

Not long after that, Abby slowly began to strengthen. She faced one major trisomy 18–related crisis after another—any of which could have been fatal—but in the face of all her difficulties, she continued to grow and to stabilize. Soon Abby was able to go home from the hospital. And when she and her parents celebrated her first birthday, even the most hardened Vegas oddsmakers would have been impressed. God had answered our prayers. Abby had done something that no one expected her to: she had lived.

Today Abby is a bright, beautiful young lady. She certainly isn't free from the effects of her trisomy 18 disorder, and she continues to face many challenges, but she's living a full life that many thought wouldn't last past its first month.

I have no doubt that our prayers played a role in Abby's recovery; only God knows just how much. It's difficult to write off the significance of a group of believers laboring in agreeing prayer over the helpless form of an infant. As far as Abby's mother is concerned, the pinpoint praying of believers was indispensable. She once commented, "I couldn't survive without prayer." I wonder if Abby would say the same thing if she could talk to us.

Who are you not praying for that you should be? Stop reading, send out a prayer email, circle the prayer wagons, and start praying for that person right now. You never know what might happen.

The Most Radical Truth about Prayer in the Bible

There's one more great reason to become a corporate pinpoint pray-er, and it may be the most important reason of all. We've looked at Matthew 18:19, in which Jesus promised that if two of us agree about what we ask, it will be given to us. Then we looked at his follow-up statement in verse 20, in which he promised that if just two believers gather in his name, he is there with them. Those verses are quite a one-two punch about the power of agreeing prayer. But have you ever noticed the verse that precedes these two? "I tell you the truth, whatever you bind on earth will be bound in heaven, and whatever you loose on earth will be loosed in heaven" (v. 18).

Whenever Jesus begins a statement with "I tell you the truth," he's raising the level of significance of what he's saying. He's stating an eternal truth and doesn't want us to miss it. These "I tell you the truth" statements are ones the King James Version translates "verily, verily." It's like Jesus is saying, "Now listen up. I need to tell you something very important, and you can't afford to miss it." What Jesus tells us, in short, is that the church and the interaction of believers is the spiritual thermostat for the entire spiritual world. In other words, as the church goes, so goes the spiritual realm.

This may seem mystical and even somewhat confusing on the surface, but it's really not so difficult to understand. In Matthew 16:19, when Jesus first made this statement, he introduced it by saying, "I will give you [the church] the keys of the kingdom of heaven." Then he added that whatever the church tied up on earth would also be restrained in the heavenly realm, and whatever the church unleashed would also be unrestrained in the spiritual realm.

It's important to note that Jesus used the word *you* in the plural. Jesus was talking to believers throughout history and all over the world; he was talking to you and me. Let me give you my not-so-sophisticated interpretation of what he was saying:

> Look, as my followers on earth, the ball really is in your court. I've basically left it up to you to determine how much of my power and authority you experience. Just think of the church as one big spiritual thermostat. Whatever you believers as a group are set on here on earth will be unleashed in the heavenly realms. If you're set on love, then love will be released all throughout the heavenly realm. If you're set on joy and unity, then those will be released as well. But if your hearts are set on hatred, conflict, and discord, then those will rule the heavenlies. I have put the keys to the kingdom of heaven in your hands. Whatever you unlock on earth is going to rule the day in the spiritual realm.

I call this concept the "satellite syndrome," because Jesus is basically saying that whatever our hearts reflect within the church will be beamed up into the spiritual world. The battle that rages in the heavenly realm will be directed and dictated by the actions, attitudes, and values of God's people on earth. But here's the scary part to that verse: whatever we beam up will be broadcast back to us a hundredfold.

When a signal is sent to a satellite up in space, it's reproduced and sent back to earth to countless receivers. It's the ultimate example of "what goes up must come down." That reality is true spiritually as well on a much more

> The battle that rages in the heavenly realm will be directed and dictated by the actions, attitudes, and values of God's people on earth.

profound level. Jesus is telling us that if we as believers are of one heart in our prayers and love for each other, then not only will that unity set the tone for the heavenly realm, but it will be poured out as a spiritual blessing all over the world. But if we're not united—if we're in conflict or we're judgmental toward each other, if we're gossipy and hateful, if we argue over our petty differences, if we're isolated and never meet as a united body of believers, and if we're prayerless—then not only will those faults be broadcast into the spiritual realm, but they'll also be rebroadcast to everyone on the earth. No wonder Jesus said he was giving us the keys to the kingdom.

What on Earth Are You Doing?

In light of these awesome spiritual realities, can you think of a better reason to become a committed corporate pray-er? Isn't it time we stopped shirking our biblical responsibility to practice agreeing prayer? Men, commit yourselves to praying with each other. Be as good at group prayer as you are at fishing or pickup basketball. Women, commit yourselves to corporate prayer. Make intercession part of your get-togethers. Couples, pray together every day. Let us not neglect the prayer opportunities in our churches. With so much power attached to the unified prayers of believers, we ought to be rearranging our schedules so that we can maximize our opportunities to pray together.

Can we afford not to? We live in an unbelievably tumultuous time in history, and who can doubt that some of the world's chaos is the direct result of our failure at intercession? Isn't the world in serious trouble today at least in part because we as the church have mismanaged the keys to the kingdom? Think about your own life.

How much time in the past seven days did you spend in pinpoint corporate praying with other Christians? How about the last month? The last year? If your answer is the same as that of most other Christians, then your actual participation in strategic group prayer is quite limited.

What would happen if Christians sold out to the concept of agreeing pinpoint prayer? What if we took seriously Jesus's teachings and started praying as if the world's condition really did depend on it? What if your city's pastors met regularly to pray for its leaders and social issues? What if parents met monthly to pray for their children's principals, teachers, and administrators? What if small groups met throughout the week to pray for their neighbors? What if believers at your job met regularly to pray for co-workers?

With all of this agreeing prayer going on, what do you think the thermostat of heaven would be set on? What would be unleashed in the spiritual realm and rained down on earth a hundredfold? We don't have to wonder. There are places around the world where Christians are meeting for pinpoint prayer just as I've described, and the outcomes are quite predictable: crime rates drop dramatically, economies flourish, gang wars end, notorious criminals come to Christ, key political figures and civic leaders openly acknowledge their faith, church attendance surges, the homeless are housed, the poor are comforted, and injustices are made right. In short, revival comes to the land.

So what about it? Are you ready to become an agreeing pray-er? Even just a few minutes a day spent in intercession with other Christians can have dramatic kingdom effects. Let's humble ourselves, repent of our superficial busyness, come together in prayer, and give God a really big target for his blessing.

Suggestions for Group Praying

Like any group setting, there is etiquette we can follow when seeking to maximize our pinpoint corporate praying. Here are some suggestions.

Don't preach. Group prayer is not the time for sermonizing. When you're praying, people aren't interested in hearing how much you know about the Bible. They don't care how many verses you can recite from memory. And they're not particularly interested in you reciting a bunch of information to God that he (and each of them) already knows. A group prayer setting isn't the place to recite the entire history of the Old Testament or to wax eloquent about the theological nuances of the Trinity. Just pray, "Father, in Jesus's name, we ask you for . . . You know better than we do what's at stake. Please hear us and answer our prayers."

Seek points of agreement. The whole point of group praying is to agree before God, so pray things with which people can agree and align their hearts. Making controversial statements or going off on some theological tangent only creates confusion. Stay simple and focused. Give the group big targets to make agreeing easy: "God, you are holy. Show yourself as holy in Carol's life. Father, we ask that you deliver Pat from his alcoholism. God, in Jesus's name, intercede and stop Joan from aborting her baby. Father, we pray that you'll comfort John in his time of sorrow." Praying with such clearly noble objectives makes agreeing easy for all involved, and that's the goal of group praying.

Pray Scripture. God's Word is the dynamite of prayer. It makes prayer explosive and powerful. There may be no more anointed form of pinpoint praying than group intercession that agrees about Scripture. Praying God's words back to him, reminding him of his promises, is very powerful praying. Add to it the agreement of other believers, and suddenly you have a spiritual sledgehammer of power that can drive away the powers of darkness. When you gather with other believers to intercede, get out your Bible and pray it back to God: "Lord, your Word says . . . Because of that, Father, we agree in asking you for . . ."

Don't dominate. I used to be part of a group that prayed together every week. We would often mention prayer requests and needs before praying. Then, inevitably, the same guy would start us off. He'd pray for every request we named in great detail. Sometimes he'd go on for twenty minutes! I used to sit and listen to the sighs of my teammates as they realized that this prayer prima donna was doing it again. In the imagery of Matthew 18, we were like a symphony with only one musician actually getting to play. It made me want to interrupt him and shout, "Hey, can we play too?" It sounded like he was praying more for show than for eternity.

It's hard to practice agreeing prayer if others don't have the chance to speak up and join in. So keep it short. State your case before God and get out of the way. Let others add to the symphony. Make beautiful prayer music—*together*.

Don't rebut. Corporate prayer is no place to work out your theological differences with other believers. Don't correct, don't counter, don't offset. Group pinpoint praying is the place for agreeing, not arguing. It's the place to fan the flames of each other's passions, not douse them.

Recently I was praying in a group for the healing of a little girl. She was very ill and facing death. The group was asking God quite passionately for her healing. I prayed and agreed with them. I asked God to do something miraculous in her life. Right after I prayed, another guy chimed in. I knew immediately that the whole prayer meeting was in trouble. From his first word, I could tell he wasn't on the same page as the rest of us. It was obvious he was neither at peace nor in agreement with what we were asking God to do. It was as if he felt the need to tone us down, to chill us out a little. In his "prayer" he was subtly saying, "Hey, guys, let's not get too carried away with this whole healing thing. We all know that God doesn't heal everyone, and he's probably not going to heal this little girl. So let's not stick our necks out too far lest we all wind up very disappointed." The prayers following that one took on a much "safer" tone.

Talk about a momentum killer! Our spirit had been quenched, the rebuke deftly delivered. It reminded me of when Jesus's power was limited in his hometown of Nazareth because of the people's lack of faith (see Matt. 13:58).

In group prayer, God is looking for community, not commentary. He wants agreement, not argument. Don't be the voice that pours water on the flame of God's Spirit in prayer. If you can't agree with the prayers, excuse yourself from the meeting. Your lack of agreement may actually be hindering the others' efforts to experience real breakthrough praying.

Agree in Jesus's name. Matthew 18:20 tells us that the most important factor in gathering and agreeing together is doing so in Jesus's name. Those words aren't just a formula we tag on at the end of a prayer. They're not just some rote religious saying. To pray in Jesus's name is to state boldly that we believe our requests are consistent with the nature and passion of Jesus. To meet in Jesus's name is to say that our agenda is consistent with the will of Jesus and that it will honor him. Prayers offered in Jesus's name are the kind that he himself would pray. Meetings held in Jesus's name are the type that he himself would attend.

When you agree in Jesus's name, you're saying that Jesus himself would agree with what is being prayed at that moment. You're believing that if Jesus were physically sitting in your prayer meeting, he would add his "Amen" to everyone else's.

When you're in a group prayer setting and something is prayed that you agree with, stop and agree right then in Jesus's name. I frequently will do this out loud, albeit quietly. I'll say, "Yes, Lord, I agree in Jesus's name." Not only does that set my heart in alignment with the others in the room, but it tells them that I'm fully engaged with them in prayer. They gain strength and encouragement from knowing that someone else is on the same page they are. And God loves it. Remember, it's into such settings of corporate agreement that God has promised to send his blessing.

Ready, Aim, Agree!

Are you ready? The thermostat of heaven is waiting for you to help determine its setting. As soon as you finish this chapter, get on your knees and commit before God to build group pinpoint praying into your life. Then become a participant in the greatest and most powerful meeting in the world—the prayer meeting. The results will be obvious.

Discussion Questions

1. When was the last time you prayed out loud with a group of Christians? Was the experience good or bad for you? How frequently do you pray with other Christians?
2. How is praying together in a group different from several Christians agreeing to pray about the same thing separately?

3. What are the most common barriers to group prayer? Why don't believers spend more time praying together?
4. Jesus placed a high premium on Christians living in unity together. How does group prayer work to increase Christian unity?
5. Describe in your own words what the "satellite syndrome" is. What evidence of it do you see in our world today?
6. What issues in your church, your city, or your life should you be praying about with other believers?
7. Based on this chapter, what could you do to build regular group prayer into your life?

FOLLOWING JESUS'S EXAMPLE
Pinpoint Praying for Your Spouse

Therefore he is able to save completely those who come to God through him, because he always lives to intercede for them.

Hebrews 7:25

I married my high school sweetheart, Susie, on June 1, 1985. We've been married more than twenty years. I have no doubt that whenever you pick up this book and read this chapter, we'll still be married. God has blessed us with a strong marriage.

Now, I'm *not* saying that our marriage is perfect. Far from it. We fight and pout and have really hard moments of marital stress. Yet in all of that, we seem to have a bond that allows us to bend but not break. The primary factor in our marriage's survival is our mutual faith in and submission to Christ—and, specifically, how that faith is manifested in our prayers.

Susie and I had a traditional June wedding. We married in a large Baptist church with dim, romantic lighting and candles. The music of Sergei Rachmaninoff, along with some of the greatest hymns of the Christian faith, helped create the mood. We exchanged traditional vows under the guidance of our lifelong pastor. But we did break with tradition in one key area: we saw each other before the ceremony. Our photographer convinced us that stress levels go down dramatically when most of the wedding pictures can be taken before the wedding, leaving only a few shots for after.

We had a blast with friends and family hamming it up together before our serious, more formal gathering. But that wasn't my first meeting with Susie on our wedding day. Before we met for photos, Susie and I had a quiet meeting alone in a private room in the church. We oohed and aahed over how we looked in our wedding garb, and then we prayed. It was a short prayer (it's difficult to be too serious about intercession when you're holding the woman of your dreams and you're about to finally marry her), but it was significant enough to remind us both of the real hope and strength in our relationship.

That prayer set the tone not just for the ceremony but for our marriage. We've prayed with each other and for each other nearly every day since. Without those daily marriage pinpoint prayers, I'm quite sure that we wouldn't be married happily, if at all. Prayer is the glue of our marriage.

We Need All the Help We Can Get

You don't need an advanced degree in sociology to know that marriage is in trouble in our culture. Statisticians tell us that the divorce rate remains alarmingly high. Crazy work schedules, financial stresses, conflicting career paths, relational baggage, emotional immaturity, sexual dysfunction, Internet pornography, high rates of infidelity, the drive for material gain, the lack of healthy spiritual input, and sometimes the added tensions that come with a failed first marriage—any of these can contribute to a Mount Everest of difficulty that married couples must climb if they are to survive.

Added to that is the unhealthy trend of cohabitation before marriage. Despite solid evidence to the contrary, many couples today—Christians included—believe that the marriage "test drive" is still a good idea. And while psychologists and sociologists consistently report that cohabitation actually decreases the chance of a marriage's success, shacking up continues to be a major part of most couples' premarital strategy.

With all this momentum working against marriage these days, we need to seek every ounce of support we can if we are serious about having fulfilling, God-honoring marriages. Without question, the most potent marriage booster is prayer. I am asking you today, whether you're married or single, to begin praying for your marriage. You can't afford not to.

The Best Praying Husband Ever

In both Testaments of the Bible, the most commonly used metaphor to describe God's relationship to his people is *marriage*. That union is the human relationship that best imitates God's covenant relationship with us. When Israel would stray from God in the Old Testament, the prophets frequently compared her to an adulterous and wayward spouse. The first three chapters of the book of Hosea portray God's love for his unfaithful people through the heartbreaking example of Hosea's marriage to a prostitute.

In the New Testament, the apostle Paul taught that the standard for husband-wife relationships was that of Christ and the church. Paul could find no higher example of love and a service-based relationship than that modeled by Christ with his bride. Jesus is presented as the ultimate spouse: he is the great husband, the ultimate lover of our souls. As such, his primary role is intercession.

In Hebrews 7:25, the writer tells us that Jesus is "able to save completely those who come to God through him, because he always lives to intercede for them." In his exalted role, Jesus spends his time interceding for you and me. I love that image. Jesus could easily spend his time lapping up the praises of the saints and angels in heaven. But there's kingdom work to be done, there are souls at stake, and there are believers in the line of fire. So Jesus prays. He's praying for you right now. That's the kind of husband he is—one whose primary work and joy is intercession for his bride.

Let me ask you some questions. How would the marriages in our culture look if husbands and wives believed that their primary role in marriage was intercession? If you're married, do you pray for your spouse? Are you interceding regularly for your marriage? Do you take your pinpoint praying role as seriously as Jesus does?

If you're single, you're not off the hook. If you intend to be married in the future, you should be praying for your spouse right now. Even if you don't yet know them, your future spouse is out there making decisions, forming values, and facing temptations. Pray for them! Start loving and fighting for your spouse in prayer even before you know their name.

The Oxygen of Marriage

Based on Jesus's example, pinpoint praying for each other is the highest and noblest role we can assume in marriage. Let's think about why prayer is so critical to the health and vitality of a marriage.

Prayer equips you to fulfill your biblical role. The assignments given to husbands and wives in the Bible are not simple. The descriptions of Christ-centered marriages in Ephesians 5 couldn't be more lofty. Without the ongoing work of the Holy Spirit in us, we'll never come close to the godliness described in the roles in Ephesians 5:22–33.

Husbands are instructed to love their wives the way Christ loves the church—the way he loves every Christian. In other words, they're supposed to die for them. Jesus set aside his rights, entitlements, and personal preferences and died for his bride, the church. That's the role model for every Christian husband. Every day he is called to die for his wife and family. No Christian husband is godly enough to do that without steady doses of marriage pinpoint prayer.

Wives are instructed to submit to their husbands in the same way that the church yields to Christ. Jesus is the perfect husband—always loving, always selfless, always safe—and therefore easy to submit to. Jesus never demands submission; rather, he allows us to give it voluntarily. Similarly, Christian wives are called to submit daily—to serve, support, honor, and yield—to their husbands. That loving submission is never forced or coerced; it's always granted joyfully and voluntarily. If husbands are called to die for their wives, then wives are called to live for their husbands just as the church lives for Jesus.

Try as we may, to live and die for each other in marriage isn't easy. I have way too much ego and selfishness

Following Jesus's Example

in me to die to my own needs and to live for Susie's. As much as I hate to admit it, I often approach serving Susie with a "what's in this for me" mind-set. Such selfishness in marriage isn't just unbiblical, it's ungodly. That's why I need daily marriage pinpoint praying. It equips me for the role I'm called to play in my marital relationship.

Consider the following example: A Christian man is driving home from a long day at work. His wife, Tina, is already home with their two kids. She's had an equally long and trying day. As he approaches their house, his thought process goes as follows: *I am so tired. I can't wait to get home. I'm going to grab some dinner and a cold drink, then plop down for an hour or two of veg time for ESPN's* SportsCenter. *Then, after Tina gets the kids down, I'll take her in the bedroom for a little sexual exercise. That should help take the edge off this otherwise ugly day.*

Now consider the same Christian man driving home after the same long day. But this time, his thought process goes differently: *Lord, I'm really tired. It's been a really ugly day. I have nothing good to offer Tina or our kids right now. Would you please replenish my spirit? I know that you want me to go home and serve my family. You want me to be fully present with my kids. You want me to pray with them before they go to sleep. You also want me to put Tina's needs before my own and to die for her. I'm sure she's had a really long day too. Would you please meet my needs right now? Would you please fill me with your Spirit so I can be a servant when I walk into my house? Equip me by your grace to do what I cannot. Thank you for helping me do what you've called me to do. Lord, I commit these next few hours to you. Help me honor you with all that happens in my home.*

That's one man with two completely different mindsets. Did you note what made the difference? It was pinpoint praying. Prayer equips you to be the husband or wife that God intended. Pray every day for God to fulfill his Ephesians 5 assignment in you. That's a marriage pinpoint prayer that God will answer.

Prayer provides perspective. It's easy to lose focus in marriage. The day in and day out of bill paying, carpooling, and honey-doing can cause even the most happily married couples to begin to feel routine. Over time, your spouse's traits and habits that didn't used to bother you can become irritating. You can easily start focusing on what's wrong or what's lacking in your spouse rather than what's good or right.

That's when you need marriage pinpoint prayer. Praying for your marriage grants you perspective that you might not gain otherwise. It takes your focus off your spouse and puts it on Christ. As a result, prayer helps you see your mate from a godly, eternal perspective.

The apostle Paul wrote about this amazing attitude adjustment in 2 Corinthians 5. His relationship with Jesus had changed how he viewed other people: "So from now on we regard no one from a worldly point of view" (v. 16). As Paul grew closer to Jesus, he found himself growing less judgmental toward others. He found he was more patient and tolerant of individuals and more compassionate toward them. He was now seeing them through Jesus's eyes instead of through the world's.

How do you view your spouse right now? Do you wish he was more understanding? Do you wish she was thinner? Do you wish he made more money? Do you wish she had fewer words? As you grow more intimate and familiar with someone, the temptation is to begin to see them from a worldly standpoint. We start to take them for granted, to respect them less, and to find them less attractive and more commonplace. Pinpoint praying changes that. It helps you refocus your perspective and see your spouse through Jesus's eyes. Once again you begin to see them as someone Jesus died for, someone Jesus is still working in, and someone you're called to serve.

As you begin to see your spouse the way God does, you'll gain God's hope for them. You'll know that God is working in them and that he still wants his best for them. You'll learn to accept your spouse and to love them without condition because that's how God accepted you. In short, the shift of perspective offered through marriage pinpoint praying will help you love your spouse with Christ's love and view them as God's property, not yours.

Prayer is free marriage counseling. Not long ago, a toilet exploded in the Davis household. A toilet explosion is a bad thing on any day. It's especially bad when the man of the house has been working on the toilet all day and promising the woman of the house that fixing it is well within his plumbing prowess. After several wasted hours and even more wasted money spent on attempted repairs by the man of the house, a toilet explosion usually doesn't sit well with the woman of the house. It certainly didn't sit well with the woman in *my* house.

Susie was so put out with me that she insisted on going with me to the store for the latest round of toilet purchases. For a guy, that's the ultimate insult. No man wants to be accompanied by his wife to the hardware store because she doesn't trust him. Talk about humiliating. All the other men just stare. But Susie insisted, and off we went in pursuit of yet another toilet solution.

I wasn't sure if the silence in the car on the way to the store was from toilet tension or just from quiet enjoyment of each other's presence. I suspected the former. Susie removed all doubt when she walked up to the sales guy in the toilet department, held up the broken toilet piece, and said, "Can you fix this? If not, we may not be able to save our marriage!" There we were in our neighborhood hardware store, seeking help for our . . . marriage.

Can you relate? It seems like the smallest details can lead to big-time stress in marriage. An exploding toilet may not be a deal breaker by itself, but add that to financial pressures, unemployment, relational tension, problems with extended family, and lack of quality time, and you can suddenly find yourself asking the sales guy in a hardware store if he can save your marriage.

That's why we need to offer nonstop pinpoint prayers for our marriages. It is the best (and cheapest) marriage counseling available to any couple. Prayer works wonders in marriages when nothing and no one else can.

When you're struggling with loving your spouse, or when the tensions are soaring in your household, you need the objective voice of the Holy Spirit to teach you and to remind you of Jesus's words.

One of the names Jesus used for his Holy Spirit was *Counselor*. The literal meaning of the name is "the one called alongside." That's what the Holy Spirit does: he comes alongside us and comforts, counsels, and guides us with the wisdom of God himself. Concerning his Spirit, Jesus promised, "But the Counselor, the Holy Spirit, whom the Father will send in my name, will teach you all things and will remind you of everything I have said to you" (John 14:26). When you pray for your marriage, the Holy Spirit will guide and instruct you.

Jesus promised that the Holy Spirit, whom he also called the *Spirit of truth*, would lead us to the truth (see John 16:13). When things are getting tough and contentious between Susie and me, I'm not particularly objective about what the truth is. I just think that my feelings are hurt or that my needs aren't being met or that I'm not being listened to. When things are that bumpy, the truth is difficult to see. That's why I need to pray—it shows me what the truth really is.

Is your marriage facing a difficult time? Are you having trouble discerning what is true from what is just emotion or a wounded ego? Before you fire off another round in your marriage conflict, stop and pray. Go to the heavenly marriage counselor and ask him to show you the truth. Prayer connects you to the Holy Spirit—he's the 24-7 marriage counselor with all the power of God at his disposal. He'll lead you to truth, humble you, remind you of Jesus's words, and guide you back into a place of calm.

Tips for Marriage Pinpoint Praying

Here are some practical and biblical suggestions for making pinpoint prayer part of your marriage.

Pray together. The couple who sat before me seemed to feel life was caving in around them. Perhaps it was. From their perspective, things could not have been worse. Both had been raised in Christian families and proudly carried the banner of "Christ-follower." Yet now, three months before their wedding, the woman was several months pregnant, and they were both suffocating in shame.

After reminding them of my favorite verse for Christians in trouble—"There is now no condemnation for those who are in Christ Jesus" (Rom. 8:1)—I asked them about their prayer habits in their relationship. They confessed rather sheepishly that they had never prayed together. Think about it: the couple had dated, been together sexually, conceived a child, and decided to get married, yet they had never prayed together. No wonder they were in trouble! They had sought marriage intimacy on all levels, but they hadn't chosen the most intimate level of marriage union—praying together.

Did you know that the intimacy a couple experiences when they pray and worship together far exceeds any level of earthly and temporal intimacy that couples enjoy? If you really want to turn up the heat and passion in your marriage, if you want to get to know your spouse's heart,

> If you really want to turn up the heat and passion in your marriage, if you want to get to know your spouse's heart, and if you want to receive God's fullness in your relationship, then pray together.

and if you want to receive God's fullness in your relationship, then pray together. Praying with your spouse and for your spouse are the two most powerful things you can do for your marriage. We've already seen how powerful corporate pinpoint prayer is. Mix in the beautiful, mystical unity of marriage, and you have one potent formula for powerful pinpoint praying. Husbands, don't let the sun set today until you've prayed with your wife. Wives, ask your husband to begin praying with you at night. Singles, make praying together part of your dating process. True marriage pinpoint praying requires praying with your mate (or potential mate), not just for him or her.

At the end of my meeting with the troubled couple, I asked them to hold hands and pray. It was one of the sweetest moments I'd witnessed in a long time. It was like watching a huge wave of grace flow over them. As their prayers and confessions flowed, all the shame and guilt was broken. In those few minutes of intercession in my office, their relationship hit an entirely new level of intimacy. Praying together does that.

Pray together at night before you go to bed. The apostle Paul wasn't joking when he commanded us to never let the sun set on our anger (see Eph. 4:26). My pastor used to say that he and his wife never went to bed angry at each other. Then he'd smile and add that sometimes they didn't go to bed for weeks! Prayer at night is a great way to ward off anger at the end of the day. If you are committed to praying together before either one of you goes to sleep, then you'll be forced to deal with any pent-up frustrations. For example, it's hard for me to pray with Susie if I'm angry at her or if I know she's put out with me. If we're serious about praying together at night—which we are—then we have to work through our garbage before we pray. Prayer helps keep our relationship free from a buildup of daily junk.

Pinpoint praying at night is also a really great way to say "I love you" to your spouse. As I'm writing this paragraph, it's after eleven at night. When Susie told me about an hour ago that she was going to bed, I set aside my work, went into the bedroom, and prayed with her. My willingness to stop working and spend a few moments interceding with her speaks volumes to Susie about my love for her. When the last thing your spouse hears at night is your voice praying for her, it's hard for her not to feel loved as she goes to sleep.

Make marriage pinpoint praying the last thing you do together at night.

Pray together over meals. This may seem obvious, but you'd be amazed how much marriage enrichment can happen with just a few spoken words in prayer before a meal. First, remember that praying together before meals requires you to eat together, and that alone will go a long way toward strengthening your marriage. But before you start to eat, pause to address the Lord together. This practice of thanking him for his gracious provision and of acknowledging your dependence on him helps create in your home an environment of prayerful humility before God. It sets a strong prayer example for your children as well.

When our son went away to college, I started praying for him at dinner with Susie and our two girls. Now they hear me pray for him at most of our dinners together. Not only am I interceding for my son, but I'm also modeling prayer for my wife and daughters.

Pinpoint praying before meals helps incorporate prayer into the routine fabric of your married life. Pray together before you eat—in restaurants, with friends, or at home—and you'll find prayer becoming a normal part of your marriage relationship.

Pray the Bible for your spouse. This is no doubt the most dramatic part of marriage pinpoint praying. It is difficult to overstate the conviction I feel about this subject. Years ago I began praying very specific biblical promises for my wife. I made my requests of God based on what both Susie and I felt were her most urgent needs.

When Susie was in middle school, she witnessed a brutal murder. For years afterward she dealt with terrible fear. She couldn't stay by herself, she went to extremes to protect herself and those she loved, and she struggled with incessant worry. Susie was a prisoner to the nightmare through which she'd lived.

Early in our marriage, I began to pray about Susie's fear issues. But rather than praying what I thought God should do for her, I simply prayed the Scriptures. Proverbs 31:25 says that a godly woman "is clothed with strength and dignity; she can laugh at the days to come." The New American Standard Bible says that "she smiles at the future." I began to pray that Susie would be clothed with strength and dignity, that she would have no fear or worry, and that she would be able to smile at the future. Verse 26 says, "She speaks with wisdom, and faithful instruction is on her tongue." I began to pray this verse for her also. I asked that God would fill her with wisdom and that her words would be laced with the faithful instruction of God's Word. Susie had always felt that God had an important ministry of teaching and writing in store for her. We both began to pray for God to equip her to fulfill that role.

What happened in the years that followed still amazes me. I watched Susie transform before my eyes. She came face-to-face with her fears. She dealt with the stronghold that witnessing a murder had created in her. She began to look to God, not people or circumstances, for her security. She started praying instead of worrying. She fell in love with the Bible and really began to take God's Word to heart. Her faith levels grew, and her spiritual wisdom and maturity increased dramatically. At some point in Susie's transformation, I recognized that God was honoring my prayers. She was clothed with strength and dignity, she was starting to smile at the future, and wise teaching was on her lips. God honors prayer, and he was honoring mine for my wife.

Now, I'm certainly *not* saying that Susie changed because of my prayers alone. Susie changed and grew because she was obedient to God's leading in her life. God led and called her to grow and to trust him, and she chose to do so. But my prayers did give momentum and power to what God was doing in Susie. Marriage pinpoint praying helped fuel the fire that God was kindling in her.

Today Susie doesn't think twice about staying alone. When I asked her if I could travel for six weeks in the Colorado mountains with our son during my sabbatical, she didn't hesitate to agree. (I think maybe she needed a break from me!) She is a secure, strong, faith-filled woman.

Susie has a national writing and speaking ministry as well. God has given her an amazing ability to communicate his Word. She travels all over the country speaking to thousands of people about the power and truths of God's Word. Watching God grow Susie has been one of the most thrilling aspects of my Christian life and certainly one of the most exciting parts of our marriage. And if Susie were writing this section, she could tell how her prayers have been equally effective in changing me.

Here are some examples of great biblical promises (all taken from Psalms) that you can pray for your spouse:

- Pray that their delight will be in the law of the Lord and that they'll meditate on his Word day and night (see Ps. 1:2).
- Ask God to be a shield about them, to bestow his glory on them, and to lift up their head (see Ps. 3:3).
- Pray that they will find their refuge in God and that he will spread his protection over them (see Ps. 5:11).
- Ask God to contend with those who contend with your mate and to fight against those who would harm them (see Ps. 35:1).
- Pray that they would love God's Word more than silver or gold (see Ps. 119:72).

Are you praying for your spouse? What are you asking God to do in them? Don't try to impose your will on God or your mate. Don't try to re-create them in your own image. Pray God's Word for them every day and trust that he will do in them what he deems necessary. There are literally thousands of promises in Psalms alone that you can pray for your spouse. You can also seek out some very specific promises to speak to their needs, as I did for Susie.

So get to it! Start praying those biblical promises for your mate. You'll see your spouse becoming more godly and holy, you'll grow closer to God as you see his amazing answers to prayer, and you'll fall more in love with your spouse as they become more of the person God intended.

No More Status Quo

My wife and I are big Nichole Nordeman fans. We love her music, specifically her poignant lyrics. She frequently says through her songs what we're thinking and feeling. In her song *Brave*, she calls Christians to no longer accept the status quo in their following of Christ. The same can be said for Christian marriage. Status quo will typically guarantee failure in any marriage. Pinpoint praying is the solution to status quo. Don't settle for the sorry excuse for marriage that culture offers. Don't get trapped in the gravitational pull of a commonplace marriage. Declare war on the status quo. Pray!

Discussion Questions

1. If you are married, how important is the role of prayer in your marriage? Rate it 1 to 5, with 5 being extremely important. If you're single and you intend to be married in the future, how much time do you spend praying for your future spouse?
2. From the example of Jesus in the New Testament, what can you learn about the significance of prayer in relationships?
3. The author argued that spiritual intimacy is the highest form of relational intimacy. Can you think of some times when you and your spouse were really connecting spiritually? What role did prayer play in your spiritual connection?

Pray Big

4. Name one thing you would like to change in your marriage. Are you praying about it? What would God say about what you need to change?
5. The author talked about how his prayers helped change his wife. Have you seen your prayers positively impact a spouse or close friend?
6. Will you pray differently for your spouse after reading this chapter? If so, how?

8

CLEAN HANDS AND A PURE HEART
Pinpoint Praying for Your Children

Then little children were brought to Jesus for him to place his hands on them and pray for them.

Matthew 19:13

It's one of the most precious keepsakes I have from my children. I keep it in my office and look at it almost every day. It's an old piece of scratch paper with a child's scribbled writing on it, and it means the world to me. Let me tell you about it.

My kids grew up hearing me pray. We made it a normal part of life in the Davis household. For our three children, *not* praying with their parents would be unusual. I have prayed with my kids before they go to sleep just about every night of their lives. When I tuck them in, I sit on the bed and say a brief prayer for them. It's not theologically profound or long and intense; it's more just an acknowledgment of Jesus's lordship in our lives and a request for his continued favor, protection, and provision. Prayer was just part of our nightly routine, right up there with brushing and flossing our teeth.

I had no idea how much these prayers meant to my kids until one night when our middle child, Emily, left me a note. I had been out late and had not made it home before Emily went to bed. When I got home, I went in to check on her. I found a piece of paper lying on top of her covers. In her childlike letters she had written, *Dad, dont furgit to pray*. Spelling and grammatical errors notwithstanding, that little note's profundity still moves me. It quickly became a motto for me as a parent—*Dad, don't forget to pray!*

Do you pray for your children? Do you know how to pray for them? A prayer offered for a child is a pinpoint prayer that we know God loves to answer. Let's see why.

The Example of Jesus

We know we're on solid footing when praying for our kids, because Jesus placed such a high premium on pinpoint prayers for children. People frequently brought their children to Jesus so he could pray for them. What amazing insight those parents had! They recognized Jesus's power and authority and knew that his holy prayers would help and benefit their kids. So they asked him to lay his hands on them, to bless them, and to pray for them.

On one such occasion, the disciples tried to stop parents from bringing their children to Christ (see Matt. 19:13). Perhaps they thought that praying for little ones was below the dignity of their leader. We don't really know what they were thinking. What we do know is that Jesus wasn't pleased with their interference. He quickly rebuked them and set them straight: "Let the little children come to me, and do not hinder them, for the kingdom of heaven belongs to such as these" (v. 14). That scene is played out repeatedly in the gospels. From it we learn that Jesus believed pinpoint praying for children is one of the noblest and most important tasks that a parent can engage in.

Head, Shoulders, Knees, and Toes

Picture your children standing before you. There are enough promises and exhortations in the Bible for you to cover your children virtually head to toe in prayer. For our purposes, we'll focus mostly on pinpoint prayers from Psalm 119, but know that there are hundreds, if not thousands, of other promises in the pages of the Bible.

Consider your children's hands. They're used for eating, practicing a musical instrument, playing video games, doing homework, and maybe even driving a car. Your children's hands help them take a shower, tie their shoes, and type on a keyboard. They're involved in just about every aspect of your children's lives. They can be used for God's glory, and they can be involved in sin. That's why you need to pray for your children's hands.

In Psalm 119:48, David talked about his hands: "I lift up my hands to your commands, which I love, and I meditate on your decrees." Picture David the shepherd under a star-filled sky. The sheep under his care are resting quietly all around him. But David isn't sleeping. He's meditating on the Mosaic law that he's been taught all his life. To him, it's not binding or restrictive; it's beautiful and liberating. As David reflects on the truth of God's law, he spontaneously sets down his shepherd's staff and raises his hands before God. It's a gesture of both praise and surrender. He prays, *Father, I lift my hands to your name. They reflect the posture of my heart.*

That's a simple pinpoint prayer that you can pray for your children. Pray that they, like David, will surrender to and worship God. Pray that they'll find his law appealing, not repulsive. Ask that their hands reflect the posture and attitude of their hearts. Pray that they might live with open and upturned hands toward God.

Now I want you to try something. (You may have to set this book down, so feel free.) Turn your hands faceup, then raise them up to about chest level. Think about this position. It's hard to do anything else really well when your hands are turned up. You can't be defensive or particularly aggressive, and you're certainly limited on the ways you can get in trouble. Basically, upturned hands are good for signaling surrender or receiving something from someone else. That's the point.

When you pray for your kids, pray that they'll live with a palms-up attitude. As they do, they'll be more likely to grow into godly and humble men and women whose hands are used for serving, caring, worship, and performing acts of righteousness, not for performing acts of sin.

Think about your children's feet. If you have young children, their feet are probably still in the "cute" stage. But as you know, feet grow—and they get stinky!

When I was in middle school, my dad drove my sister and me from Austin to Arkansas so we could compete in a water skiing tournament. On the ride home, after several hours of being cramped in the backseat of our Buick and being stuffed into hot sneakers all day, my feet needed a little break. I quietly slipped off my shoes and peeled down my rather sticky socks. I wiggled my toes and relished the moment of my newfound foot freedom. We were traveling at night, so no one was aware of what I was doing—at least not initially. But then a strange, deathlike aroma began to fill our car. My sister, who had been sleeping, woke up and asked, "What is that smell?" My dad knew. He pulled the car off the road, opened all the windows and doors, ordered me

> When you pray for your kids, pray that they'll live with a palms-up attitude.

to put my shoes back on, and proceeded to lecture me on the finer points of social etiquette and when shoe removal was appropriate, which, in my case, was never.

Feet need prayer. But not just because they get smelly. They need prayer because they support us and carry us into whatever we're doing. David talked about his feet. He knew that his feet could take him up and down mountain terrain; support him in a fight with a lion, a bear, or a Philistine; and carry him into a place of worship or a house of sin. He knew his feet could easily be tripped up and cause him to stumble, so he prayed for them: "Direct my footsteps according to your word; let no sin rule over me" (Ps. 119:133).

You can pray that same promise for your children's feet. Ask God to direct your children's every step. Pray they'll be so submitted to God, so true to his will, that their paths will always be consistent with his Word. Pray that the Bible would be the script your children closely follow, the instruction manual for how they live. Ask God to guide them every day according to the teachings of his Word and to protect them from straying outside the safety of his commands. Pray, like David, that no sin will ever rule or have dominion over them. Ask God to give them courage to run away from sin when they are tempted.

David prayed for his feet again in Psalm 119:105 when he said, "Your word is a lamp to my feet and a light for my path." He asked that God's Word be the light that guided him along the perilous paths of life. Ask God the same for your kids. Pray that his Word will illuminate their paths. Pray that they'll trust in, believe in, and commit to memory the teachings of the Bible. Ask God to use

Clean Hands and a Pure Heart

his Word to keep your children on the path to holiness. That's a pinpoint prayer God will answer.

Look into your children's eyes. Think about what they see. I'm not talking about what they see when they look at you; you're probably a very safe and comforting image. I want you to think about what they see every day when they're not with you—the computer images, photos, and billboards.

You know that what we look at can have a huge impact on our lives. I said in the previous chapter that my wife witnessed a murder when she was in middle school. What she saw wounded her terribly. Our eyes can see bright, brilliant, and inspiring sights, and they can look upon horrible things. They can gaze at things that cause us to love God more, and they can linger on things that actually destroy the knowledge of God in us. Pray for your children's eyes.

David prayed for his eyes in Psalm 119:37: "Turn my eyes away from worthless things." I'm not sure what David would have thought was worthless in his day, but I know there are plenty of worthless sights today. I can still remember the first pornographic image I saw. I was in sixth grade when a friend showed me a foldout from *Playboy* magazine. That picture would no doubt be considered benign by today's standards, but to my young and rather sheltered mind, it was shocking. I thought about it for days afterward, and most tragically, it made me want to see more.

It doesn't have to be something as dramatic and worthless as sexually explicit material to attract your children's attention. There are plenty of other worthless things they can set their eyes on. Consider the pull of material possessions. Our culture has expertise in making stuff look attractive and important to children. And what about popularity? Kids can either long for what popular students have or begin to think they're not as valuable because they're not as popular. Kids also look at all types of printed material, television, Internet, and multimedia that can be very alluring. The messages these media send to our children aren't always God-honoring and can be very damaging. We need to pray that our children have the discernment to recognize dangerous or damaging material and the courage to turn away from it.

What are your children looking at? What worthless things have worked their way into their field of vision? Pray for their eyes! Pray that God will protect them from harmful and addicting sights. Pray that when tempted, your kids will turn their eyes away from the worthless and back toward the righteous. Pray that they'll set their gaze, spiritual and literal, on Jesus and that they would be repulsed by any image that dishonors his name.

Please cover your mouth! Another area to cover in prayer is your children's mouths. James warned us about our mouths:

> All kinds of animals, birds, reptiles and creatures of the sea are being tamed and have been tamed by man, but no man can tame the tongue. It is a restless evil, full of deadly poison. With the tongue we praise our Lord and Father, and with it we curse men, who have been made in God's likeness. Out of the same mouth come praise and cursing. My brothers, this should not be.
>
> James 3:7–10

How many times has your mouth gotten you in trouble? I can't even begin to count the number of times my errant words or slips of the tongue have produced relational chaos in my world. What about you? How many times have you had to apologize for or explain a word you've spoken? How many times have you made promises you couldn't keep, exaggerated about something, or simply lied, only to have to eat your words later? Our mouths can get us in serious trouble. And if that's true for us as adults, it's even truer for our children.

David understood how much damage his mouth could cause, so he asked God to bless his words. In Psalm 119:43, David asked that his mouth be filled with truth. He wasn't praying simply that he wouldn't lie, although that's certainly a noble and important prayer for people trying to honor God with their lips. David was praying also that he'd be committed simply to speaking the truth—no fibs, no white lies, no fudging, no gossip, no slander, no verbal abuse. Basically, he prayed that God would allow only truth to abide on his lips. His hope for maintaining his verbal high road was his constant meditation on God's Word. He wrote, "Do not snatch the word of truth from my mouth, for I have put my hope in your laws" (Ps. 119:43).

David believed that whatever went into his heart would flow back out of his mouth, so he fed himself a strict diet of God's commands. He contemplated, reflected on, memorized, and internalized them. He bombarded his mind with God's teachings in the hopes that no errant thought would be allowed in or out. David prayed that as he learned the truth of God's commands, he would always be committed to speaking it. He wanted to be a truth teller, a truth promoter, a truth messenger. He asked God to help him always speak the truth.

What a great pinpoint promise to pray for your children! How many times in a day are your children tempted to fib, to exaggerate, or to mislead? Pray that God will fill their mouths totally with truth. In doing so, you'll be addressing two very important needs they have. First, you'll be praying against deception. We all know how easy it is to let little lies and half-truths creep into our communication. Your pinpoint prayers for your children's mouths will help them fight the temptation to lie. Second, you'll be praying for your children's commitment to the truth. Truth telling is more than just not lying; it's being authentic. Truth telling is what Jesus was speaking of when he said that our *yes* should mean "yes," not "maybe" or "possibly" or "I hope so." When you pray that truth will never leave your children's mouths, you're asking God to help them be authentic and people of integrity.

David wrote another intriguing thing about his mouth. He confessed that with it he panted for God's commands (see Ps. 119:131). I can picture David out in the fields on a hot day. As he watches over his sheep, one of his trusty sheepdogs is nearby. As David takes a sip from his water pouch, he notices that his dog is panting. He's obviously hot and thirsty, longing for water. David thinks about that image and then prays, *Lord, I thirst for you. I pant for you. Help me to always long for your Word.*

What are your kids thirsting for? What will they pant after in the future? Pray that they'll have an insatiable desire for God. Ask God to draw them, to woo them, and to speak to them. Pray that your kids will constantly pant for the love and presence of their God and that they'll speak only what is true.

"Love the Lord . . . with all your mind." There is a war being waged right now for our children's minds, so we need to pray for them. The Bible teaches that the mind is the key to the soul. God reveals himself to the hearts of people through the vehicle of their minds. Thinking, reasoning, meditating—they're all part of the process of discovering God.

Every day our children are assaulted by a myriad of messages that try to negate God. Our culture is doing its best to convince the next generation that they are cosmic accidents, that morality is relative and therefore not particularly useful, that authority should be disregarded, and that their value is defined by their friends, wealth, power, sexuality, and looks. This onslaught of mental terrorism is relentless, polished, and persuasive. Kids who don't know better can quickly fall prey to its lies. That's why we need to practice pinpoint praying for the minds of our children.

In Psalm 119:99–100, David offered us an interesting approach to praying for our children's intellect. While reflecting on his own wisdom, he wrote, "I have more insight than all my teachers. . . . I have more understanding than the elders." Those are some rather audacious claims, especially if David was still relatively young when he wrote Psalm 119. But David expressed the precise mental reality we want for our kids. He was saying he was wiser than his own instructors and could outthink those who were trying to persuade or influence him.

Shouldn't we pray for our kids to be as mentally well-trained as David when they enter the hostile territory of the world? Wouldn't you love to know they can outreason the very forces that are determined to lead their minds astray? Think of your children as young men and women who know how to recognize the lies and false advertising of today's culture. Picture them as fully equipped Christ-followers who know how to offset society's sales pitches with biblical reality, and then start praying to that end.

How did David get so wise? How did he become smarter and more insightful than his teachers? He tells us the answer in verse 99: "I meditate on your statutes." David gained his wisdom and knowledge from a steady dosage of God's Word. He made it his practice to reflect on it throughout the day. As a result, his mental capabilities soared, and he grew much more insightful than the scribes and scholars of his day.

> Pray that your children will fall in love with God's Word and will learn at an early age to meditate on the truths of the Bible.

146

The Bible teaches that true wisdom, learning, and knowledge begin with a healthy reverence for God. Those who honor and love God will have levels of reasoning, creative capacities, and mental processing that those who reject God will not. Faith in God allows humble men and women to think at higher levels. And faith in God is fueled and strengthened by steady reflecting on his Word.

As parents, we need to make sure our kids are well-exposed to the life-giving principles of the Bible. We need to create an incubating environment where the seeds of the truth in God's Word can be planted deep in our children's hearts and minds. Then we need to water those seeds with pinpoint prayers. Ask God to speak to your children's minds. Pray for your children to have great wisdom, insight, and reasoning capacities. Pray that your children will fall in love with God's Word and will learn at an early age to meditate on the truths of the Bible. Such pinpoint praying will not only make them wiser and godlier, but it will equip them to rebuff the onslaught of anti-God bias that will assault them as they venture into the world.

Are you beginning to get the picture? Do you see how easy and effective it can be to pray for your children? There are hundreds of verses in the Bible that address our minds, eyes and ears, hands and feet, wills, emotions, and passions. Make it your practice to scour the Bible for these verses, and then begin to pray them regularly for your children. As you do, you'll be covering your kids head to toe in prayer. And as your children mature and grow, the results of your faithful pinpoint praying will be obvious.

Above All Else, Guard Your Heart

In the later months of 1999, ESPN began airing a sports countdown show featuring the top fifty U.S. athletes of the twentieth century. Think about that: ESPN executives and writers had the daunting task of singling out the top sports performers of the last one hundred years. Names such as Babe Zaharias, Bob Beamon, Babe Ruth, Willie Mays, Kareem Abdul-Jabbar, Magic Johnson, Jesse Owens, Muhammad Ali, Sugar Ray Leonard, Bruce Jenner, Mary Lou Retton, Tony Dorsett, Emmitt Smith, Mark Spitz, Wilt Chamberlain, Gale Sayers, Michael Jordan, and Lance Armstrong were just a few of the hundreds of athletic heroes whom the producers had to evaluate and rank. The show played to great ratings and provided countless thrilling moments of relived sports history.

There were many surprises on the list, but none greater than the athlete ranking thirty-fifth in the countdown, ahead of such sports legends as multiple Wimbledon winner Pete Sampras, New York Yankees player Mickey Mantle, and Chicago Bears Hall of Fame running back Walter Payton. This athlete was never paid a penny for his breathtaking performances. In fact, he wasn't human at all. Spot number thirty-five went to a horse: Secretariat, the only animal on the list and the winner of the 1973 Triple Crown.

I was in middle school when Secretariat captivated our nation's attention. I remember seeing his picture on the covers of *Time* and *Newsweek* in the same week. He won the Kentucky Derby and the Preakness Stakes races in dramatic, come-from-behind fashion. At Churchill Downs, Secretariat still holds the track record for the Derby. He ran the fastest time ever recorded at the Preakness as well, but he wasn't given the record because of an official timing malfunction.

As the Belmont Stakes approached, a frenzied sense of expectation swept through our nation. Americans knew they were seeing something special. Speculation grew that Secretariat would not only win the Triple Crown but would do so in record fashion.

No one was prepared for what that amazing animal did in the Belmont, a grueling mile-and-a-half sprint. Secretariat exploded from the gates and quickly sprinted to the lead, setting a blistering pace. Coming out of the first turn, he and his closest competitor, Sham, pulled away from the field. (Sham, an incredible horse in his own right, had the terrible misfortune of having to continually race against one of the greatest horses in history.) By the final turn of the race, Secretariat had pulled away from Sham and was on his way to history. He crossed the finish line alone, a whopping 31.5 lengths (the length of a football field) ahead of second place. He set track and world records that day and clearly established himself as one of the greatest race horses of all time. Not long after the Belmont, Secretariat stopped racing and enjoyed a long and peaceful retirement.

After his death in 1989, doctors performed an autopsy on the superhorse. They wanted to study his physiology and see if they could find any clues as to why he ran so well. What they found explained everything. Secretariat had a huge heart—literally. A normal horse's heart weighs about seven pounds. Secretariat's weighed twenty-two. His heart was three times larger than usual, and thus with every beat it sent three times the amount of blood and oxygen coursing through the thoroughbred's veins. Doctors also discovered that his abnormal heart size resulted from a genetic defect that could be traced through his parents and grandparents. Secretariat was able to run like he did because of his huge heart—a gift that was passed on from the generations before him.[4]

Let me ask you a question: what kind of heart are you passing on to your children? In the same way that we can pass on physical traits to our kids, we can also pass along our spiritual traits. Determine today to give the gift of a healthy spiritual condition to your kids. Determine to pass on to them a healthy spiritual heart.

David knew all about the importance of the heart. He mentioned the heart ninety-eight times in his prayers in the Psalms. He knew that the condition of the heart dictates our actions and attitudes. In Psalm 119:32, David gave us a great pinpoint promise that we can pray for our children's hearts: "I run in the path of your commands, for you have set my heart free." I love the way the New American Standard Bible words this verse. In true Secretariat imagery it says, "I shall run the way of Your commandments, for You will enlarge my heart."

In David's day, long-distance communication required runners to relay messages. Kings and generals would dispense runners from the battlefield to communicate strategies and news of wins and losses. Sometimes a general would send out two runners to the same place via different routes, in case one route was blocked or one runner was injured or captured. David drew on the imagery of battlefield runners in verse 32. He understood that the path or route he had chosen to run through life was the way of God's commands. He knew it was the safest and most secure road through the perils of life. I can imagine David praying, *Holy God, whatever I'm asked to do in your name, wherever you ask me to run, I will always take the high road laid out in your commands. Therein is the life and safety that you alone can offer.*

Consider David's reasoning: "for you have set my heart free." What a statement! David found joy and peace in the way set by God's commands. He didn't view them as binding or restrictive. His heart had been set free by the very laws against which so many of us push and complain. He had discovered that the path to freedom wasn't in independence from God but in humble and joyful submission to him. For David, the way of God's commands was the way of true freedom.

Now let's talk about your children's hearts. Are they in good condition? Are they in tune with spiritual realities? Are your children beginning to understand sin? Do they yet sense God's great love for them? Pray for your children's spiritual intuition. Ask God to make them spiritually discerning and highly aware of the spiritual realities of our world. Pray that their hearts would be sensitive to God's presence and leading.

Are your children learning to love God's Word? Are they gaining an appreciation for the life-giving aspects of God's truth? If you're seeking a church home, look for a place where God's Word is taught by gifted teachers in an age-appropriate manner. Read the Bible to your kids at night before they go to bed, especially while they're still young. But most of all, pray that they will love God's Word and hide it in their hearts. Ask God to give them a passion and hunger for the truths of his Word.

In Proverbs 4:23, Solomon told us to guard our hearts above all else, for the heart is the wellspring of life. In light of this passage, it's hard to overstate the importance of praying for your children's hearts. Start today praying the pinpoint promise that David showed us in Psalm 119:32. Pray they'll see God's laws as freeing, not binding. Ask God to help them run the path of integrity he has set out before them. Pray they will be men and women of the high road who are totally committed to walking in the way of God's commands. Think about the powerful image of Secretariat and his huge heart and then pray your kids will have an equally huge heart for God and his Word.

Let's Pray

We need to pray these pinpoint prayers every day for our children. Will you pray them with me now?

Holy Father, we ask you to pour out your favor on our sweet children. Jesus, we bring them to you through holy intercession, asking you to place your hands on them and intercede for them.

We pray for their hands. Let them be engaged in acts of giving, ministry, and service. Keep them free from acts of sin. Teach them to raise their hands to you in worship and surrender. More importantly, teach them to live in a posture of worship and surrender.

We pray for our children's feet. O Lord, keep them clean and pure. May our children be quick to run toward ministry and opportunities to serve others. May they also be quick to flee from temptation. May their feet be accustomed to traveling the high road. Teach them to walk firmly in your ways. Make them surefooted; let them not be tripped up by sin.

Father, we pray for their mouths. Let them speak only what is true. Keep our children free from all forms of spoken sin—exaggeration, boasting, lying, gossip, slander, cursing, overpromising, criticism, and inauthenticity. May they be fully committed to the truth. Train them by your Spirit to always speak truth in love. We pray also that our kids would be hungry and thirsty for your Word. Let them pant and long for the promises of your holy Scriptures.

Mighty God, we pray for our children's minds. Teach them to think critically and creatively. May you lead them to wisdom and show them truth. Make them discerning. Please teach them to love your Word and train their minds to think biblically.

O Father, protect their eyes. Protect them from the many vile and worthless images that assault them every day. Teach them to turn away from looking at wickedness. Please protect them from seeing violence and carnality that would wound their souls. Bombard their eyes with that which is true, holy, pure, and worthy of praise.

And finally, Father, we pray for our children's hearts. Expand their hearts. Make them soft soil. Please use your Word to grow and strengthen them. Teach our children *to run the way of your holy commands. Help them see that life and freedom are found in the blessed commands of your Word. O Father, let them run in freedom and joy because they are committed to your teachings.*

We pray all this for our sweet kids. Please cover them from head to toe. In Jesus's awesome name. Amen.

Discussion Questions

1. Think about how you pray for your children. What types of things do you typically pray for them?
2. Have you ever used your Bible as a guide for praying for your children? Can you think of any verses that state in clear terms what you would love to see God do in your children?
3. What is your biggest concern, worry, or fear for your kids today? How could you turn it into a pinpoint prayer? What verses of the Bible could you turn into prayers about it?
4. Think about your heart. What spiritual legacy are you passing on to your children? How might your prayers change what they are inheriting from you?
5. Based on this chapter, how will you change the way you pray for your children?

9

IT'S OKAY TO ASK

Pinpoint Praying for Yourself

I pray . . . for me.
Romans 1:10

van McGuire lived in the exciting and dangerous world of professional skydiving. His job was not only to hurl his body from a plane toward the earth at over a hundred miles per hour, but also to instruct others on how to do the same. Ivan McGuire was a professional skydiving instructor. He was so skilled at his profession that he became an instructor of other instructors. McGuire actually filmed other teachers and students in freefall and then used the footage to later evaluate an instructor's performance while in the air.

By the spring of 1988, he had over eight hundred jumps to his credit. That's the same as jumping from an airplane every day for over two years. So it was obviously no big deal when McGuire dove headlong from an airplane with camera in hand in early April 1988, ready to film another lesson. The video he shot that day told the story.

The other instructor and student were seen freefalling for several seconds before disappearing quickly from view as they pulled their respective parachute releases and their chutes deployed. The video showed McGuire's right hand moving down to pull his own release. But something clearly went wrong. Instead of the expected jerk and sudden deceleration, McGuire continued to accelerate. The film became blurry and bumpy as he struggled in the air, but the inevitable was obvious on the video. He was falling toward the earth at nearly 150 miles per hour, and he had no way to stop himself.

The final few seconds of the tape were destroyed on impact. McGuire's body was found in some woods just over a mile from the airfield. He was not wearing a parachute; he had forgotten to take it.[5]

Are You Ready to Jump?

Now consider my friend Stephen. His résumé reads like a Who's Who in the business world. Stephen has been president and/or CEO of several large and successful companies. His forte is transitioning a midsized, moderately productive company into a large, world-class organization. Then Stephen leaves, cashes in on his shares, and makes out like a bandit in the process. His leadership and transitional skills have netted him a small fortune over the years.

Stephen is also a Christ-follower. But Stephen's business savvy has not followed him into his Christian walk. He has, I believe, a fatal flaw in his discipleship process: Stephen rarely prays for himself. Stephen and I have talked at length about this spiritual idiosyncrasy. Like many other Christ-followers, he feels it is selfish to

> Jesus believed in and practiced pinpoint praying for himself.

pray for himself. He leaves his spiritual growth and pilgrimage up to God and prays only for others.

While Stephen's prayer strategy may seem noble on the surface, it's actually quite imperiling. In fact, it's the spiritual equivalent of jumping out of an airplane without a parachute. When you make the daily dive into a world of sin, temptation, mixed messages, and spiritual chaos, you'd better be fully prepared. The daily protection, discernment, and guidance you need are accessed primarily through prayer—by specific pinpoint praying for yourself. Without it, you're guaranteed to fall hard.

So here's a confession: the person I spend the most time pinpoint praying for is *me*. I'm not being selfish or immature. The person with the most immediate capacity to negatively impact my walk with Christ, to short-circuit God's kingdom work in my life, and to bring harm and chaos into the lives of the people I love the most is . . . me! That's why I spend so much time praying about me and for me. I can't afford not to. Neither can you.

Great Examples to Follow

We have only to look as far as the New Testament to find that interceding for oneself is both biblical and necessary. The Bible paints pictures of Jesus frequently withdrawing to pray, and he wasn't praying just for the people in his ministry. Jesus believed in and practiced pinpoint praying for himself.

One day while in Capernaum, Jesus ministered late into the evening healing the sick. It must have been an exhausting day for him. But very early the next morning, "while it was still dark, Jesus got up, left the house and went off to a solitary place, where he prayed" (Mark 1:35). When Peter and the other disciples finally found him, they were excited because a crowd was already gathering to see Jesus. But instead of staying there, Jesus told them that it was time to move on to other villages.

How did Jesus know that? How did he resist the temptation to become an overnight sensation through his amazing healing ministry? How did he draw the strength to face yet another day of travel, teaching, and grueling ministry? He did it through prayer—specifically, prayer for himself. Luke affirmed, "Jesus often withdrew to lonely places and prayed" (Luke 5:16).

The most obvious example of Jesus's praying for himself is found in the hours before his death. John 17 is Jesus's longest recorded prayer in the New Testament. It opens with Jesus interceding for himself. In his pinpoint prayer, he asked that he be glorified as God's Son. Jesus wasn't being selfish or egocentric when he prayed for the Father to glorify him. He knew he was within God's will, and he didn't hesitate to ask for what God intended.

A few hours later, we find Jesus in his most intense hour of self-intercession. He exhorted his disciples to stay awake and to pray with him. "Going a little farther, he fell with his face to the ground and prayed, 'My Father, if it is possible, may this cup be taken from me. Yet not as I will, but as you will'" (Matt. 26:39). Jesus shows that it is perfectly normal for us to wrestle with God over very personal issues. He shows us that we can plead with God to work directly in our lives to produce certain desired outcomes. More importantly, he shows us that when we pray for ourselves, we need to be ready to submit to God's will.

The apostle Paul is another great example of a biblical leader who frequently sought prayer and prayed for himself. Paul was a great intercessor, and his letters are filled with prayers for the church. But he also took quite seriously his need to pray for his life and ministry. Here are just a few examples.

- In Romans 1:10, Paul prayed for the opportunity to travel to Rome and serve the church there.
- In Romans 15:31, he called on the church in Rome to pray he might be delivered from the unbelievers in Judea and freed to travel to Jerusalem.
- In 2 Corinthians 12:7–8, he interceded and wrestled with God on three separate occasions for God to remove his "thorn in the flesh."
- In Ephesians 6:19, he asked the church in Ephesus to pray specifically for him and his boldness in communicating the gospel.
- In 1 Thessalonians 5:25, he wrote, "Brothers, pray for us."

I love that last verse. It sums up the heart of the Christian disciple who is neither too proud nor too independent to seek the prayers of his fellow believers. Paul knew the power of prayer. He wanted as many Christians as possible praying for him, including himself.

Finally, have you thought about David and the countless examples of his personal pinpoint prayers in the Psalms? The next time you read Psalms, mark how many times you see the words *I*, *me*, or *mine* in the text. David prayed extensively for his wisdom, his protection, his integrity, his heart, his obedience, and his morality. He prayed that he would love God's Word and hate sin. He asked that God would keep him from evil and lead him on the high road of righteousness. David was relentless when it came to praying for himself.

Are you starting to get the point? It is obvious we need to be busy about praying for ourselves.

Duh!

I read a *Wall Street Journal* article recently about a medical study, and it made me actually laugh out loud. A major university studied the sleep patterns of patients in hospitals and determined (are you ready for this profound insight?) that patients actually sleep better with less outside noise! Researchers required a significant investment of time and resources to conclude that patients in hospitals sleep better when buzzers aren't buzzing, bells aren't ringing, IV machines aren't beeping, and doors aren't opening and closing all around them. When I read the article, I said out loud, "You needed a study to figure that out?"

The same is true when it comes to praying for yourself: you shouldn't need a university study to know how important it is. It's obvious. Next to the Holy Spirit, no one knows your heart better than you. No one knows your struggles, your fears, your secret sins, your ambitions, or your needs better than you do. No one can impact your world for good or bad quite like you can. That's why you need pinpoint prayers for yourself. Duh!

Who's in Charge Here?

I'm hoping you don't still need to be convinced to pray for yourself. By now you're probably starting to see the importance and urgency of self-intercession. So, instead of spending more time making the case for personal pinpoint praying, let's move on to the practical application of it.

The most important factor in praying for yourself is what I call "settling the question of your will," or answering the "who's in charge here?" question. It's what Jesus modeled for us when he prayed in the Garden of

> Tell God the answer is yes even before you know what the assignment is.

Gethsemane for the Father's will over his own. In other words, don't approach God in prayer so you can negotiate with him. Don't waste time praying about things that are clearly unbiblical. Rather, pray what you know God wants; pray what you know he will bless. When in doubt, yield in prayer to his will no matter what.

How many times have you sought God's will in prayer so you could decide whether you intended to obey it? Why bother doing that? God won't waste time showing you great and mighty things if all you're going to do is form a committee or call a meeting to discuss them. Tell God the answer is yes even before you know what the assignment is. That's what it means to settle the question of your will. It means you've closed the door on negotiations with God. You tell him you're in, no matter what the mission is or how difficult it will be. That's the kind of pinpoint praying God will answer.

How to Pray for Yourself

Here are seven great pinpoint promises you can pray for yourself. They're biblical, they're specific, they're powerful, they're practical, and they're clearly on the right side of the "who's in charge here?" question. Pray these promises for yourself every day, and you'll soon find that you're enjoying off-the-charts levels of joy and kingdom impact.

Personal prayer #1—*Lord, help me hate sin.* I met with my accountability partner recently. We meet every two weeks to check in on our morality, spiritual conditions, family lives, and overall obedience levels. We've been in an accountable relationship together in a group or one-on-one setting for over a decade. I have no problem getting totally honest with this guy. He knows everything about me.

I confessed to him that I don't hate sin. I want to, I really do, but there's far too much of it that I still find alluring. Now, don't get me wrong; there's plenty of sin I do hate. I hate injustice and the abuse of the poor. I hate prejudice and murder. I hate it when the strong take advantage of the weak and when the name of God is mocked. There's plenty of sin I hate. But as I reflect on that, I seem to hate only the sins other people are committing. When it comes to the sins I wrestle with—stuff like pride, lust, slander, judgmental thoughts, anger, poor stewardship of my time and talents, skimping on quiet times—I'm not so quick to play the hate card. In fact, I still find many of my sins to be quite alluring. I don't hate sin, not really.

But I'm not giving up on this prayer. I've been praying for years that I would be repulsed by sin. Let's face it—sin, specifically *my* sin, is the thing that killed Jesus. So why should I love, tolerate, or cling to the very thing that cost Jesus his life? I know I should hate it, and I've been praying to that end for years. And it's working, albeit slowly. There's still far too much of it that doesn't bother me nearly enough.

How about you? Do you hate your sin? Are there certain behaviors that have a grip on you? Pray that you'll hate the very thing that currently controls you. That's a prayer God will answer.

King David gave us a great biblical basis for this prayer when he wrote that a rebellious man "flatters himself too much to detect or hate his sin" (Ps. 36:2). Have you done that? I certainly have thought way too highly of myself to take my sin seriously. It's like I'm God's grand exception to the law of sin and death in the universe.

So in light of David's insight, pray, *Lord, help me to not think too highly of myself. Help me to hate my sin. Let me see it for what it really is—that which killed your Son. O God, I pray that my sin would sicken and repulse me. And I pray this all in Jesus's holy name.*

Personal prayer #2—*Lord, help me love prayer.* Years ago I traveled to San Antonio to meet with a friend and spiritual mentor. While we enjoyed a lunch of great Mexican food, we caught up on each other's lives and ministries. Later, with full stomachs and warm hearts, we walked out of the restaurant to say our farewells and head our respective ways. But my mentor wasn't quite finished with me. He asked me to join him in his old, beat-up Ford Bronco for a few moments of prayer. I gladly complied. Those few moments marked me forever.

My mentor asked God for something I had never heard before. He prayed that I would love to pray. He prayed that I would enjoy praying. He prayed that it would be easy for me to pray. His words blew me away. I had never before thought about praying about my prayer life. But I've been praying about it ever since.

The prophet Isaiah spoke an amazing promise to Gentiles who embraced the God of Israel: God would bring them to his holy mountain (a metaphor for his holy presence) and would make them joyful in his house of prayer (see Isa. 56:6–7). What a beautiful image! For many of us, prayer is drudgery, work, and flat-out boring. Most Christians would rather endure a root canal than be forced to spend an hour in prayer. But it doesn't have to be that way. Prayer doesn't have to be an hour of hard labor.

Start praying for God to help you love prayer. Use the language of Isaiah and ask God to make you joyful in his house of prayer. God will honor your request. I know, because over the last twenty years he has answered mine. I can trace my desire to pray and my joy in prayer all the way back to those few moments in that Bronco. God honored my mentor's prayers for me, and he's been honoring mine ever since.

O God, give me a heart of prayer. Let prayer be easy for me. Help me see it as a joy, not labor, and a privilege, not a chore. Precious God, do as your Word promises. Make me joyful in your house of prayer!

Personal prayer #3—*God, give me a platform.* This is a great, practical pinpoint prayer for your career and ministry. Pray you'll be really good at whatever you spend the bulk of your time doing. Pray you'll be so good that you gain a platform through it from which you can glorify God.

Solomon talked about excellence in Proverbs: "Do you see a man skilled in his work? He will serve before kings; he will not serve before obscure men" (Prov. 22:29). I began praying this verse for my life and ministry recently after a friend pointed it out to me. I've been praying that I will be highly skilled at what I do and that God will give me a platform from which I can declare his praises.

Mediocrity never honors God. He is neither average nor mediocre, and he won't accept such low levels of output from his blood-bought children. He expects and deserves more.

Are you skilled at what you do? Do you honor and glorify God in your career and personal ministry? Pray this pinpoint promise for your life. Ask God to give you the skill to excel in your career. Pray he'll lead you to the right job so you can truly thrive and bring him honor. Then ask him for a platform. Pray he will increase your influence and impact. In the words of Proverbs, pray you might "serve before kings."

Holy Father, please make me great at what I do. Give me exceptional skill and ability so I might glorify your name. And, Father, I ask you for a platform. Increase my audience; increase my impact. Give me favor before lead-

ers. Strategically place me so I might truly honor and exalt your name.

Personal prayer #4—*Father, please give me the gift of brokenness.* (Warning: praying this may result in serious unsettling of your comfort zones and status quo. Pray it at your own risk!) Jesus taught that brokenness was at the center of kingdom living. In his opening statement of the Sermon on the Mount, Jesus promised that the poor in spirit were blessed because they uniquely possessed God's kingdom (see Matt. 5:3). The spiritual poverty that Jesus described is what I call the gift of brokenness.

Physically impoverished people can't boast or be self-reliant. They're completely dependent upon outside help and support for their daily sustenance. Spiritually impoverished people—the poor in spirit—know they have no leverage before God. They know their souls are bankrupt and their only hope is a daily wave of grace and mercy from the Father. To those broken and needy people who know they can't flash their spiritual résumés before God, Jesus promised the kingdom.

Are you broken? Do you understand that your potential in God's kingdom lies not in your ability to impress God but rather in his ability to forgive and favor you? Broken people have come to the end of themselves and have reached the freeing place of total dependence on the grace and power of God.

My friend Dave Busby, who now resides in heaven, taught me all about brokenness. Dave had cystic fibrosis. He was a forty-year-old husband, father, and minister who functioned with lungs that were only 10 percent operational. Every breath Dave took was a huge labor for him. He was—at least physically—a weak shell of a man. But Dave was one of the mightiest Christ-followers I've ever known. His physical weakness drove him to God every day for strength and mercy. God used Dave all over the world to help men and women understand his goodness. Dave was a true kingdom warrior—because he was completely broken.

Are you willing to pray the dangerous prayer for brokenness? Are you ready to ask God to shatter your status quo and to remove every physical, emotional, and material crutch that might keep you from fully relying on him? Don't be afraid of this sweet gift. Brokenness will teach you more about God's grace and mercy than living in your own strength and abilities ever could. It will make you a truly mighty citizen in God's kingdom.

O God, I humbly ask for the gift of brokenness. Please shatter anything in me that would keep me from depending on you.

Personal prayer #5—*Father, please give me your heart for lost people.* The longer we walk with Christ, the easier it is to forget what it was like to be lost. Believers have the incredible opportunity to enjoy strong Christian community. Not only do we worship with other believers, but many of us also immerse ourselves in fully Christian environments. Our kids go to Christian schools, we vacation with Christian friends, we join Christian sports leagues, we listen to Christian music, and we do business with Christian businesses. And all of this is good. However, one possible negative side effect is that we can lose contact with people who aren't Christians. Not only do we lose evangelistic opportunities, but we begin to distrust and even dislike nonbelievers. They become the enemy. For many of us, unbelieving people personify what's wrong with our culture.

Such thinking could not be farther from the heart of Jesus. The Gospels give us multiple accounts of Jesus's loving, praying for, and hanging with the very people whom many of us today would write off. Jesus didn't view lost people as the bad guys; they were the very people he came to reach. And don't forget, you used to be one of them.

How's your heart for unbelievers? Do you love them or disdain them? Do you avoid them or seek them out? If your heart is cold toward irreligious people, then at some point it has grown cold toward God.

Pray for a heart that loves and cares for the lost. Pray for compassion for their spiritual condition. Pray to love them like Jesus does.

Precious God, thank you for not writing me off when I was without you. Help me not to ignore those for whom you died. Give me your heart and your love for the very people you came to save. Forgive me for my "club" mindset. Please keep my heart soft and compassionate toward unbelievers.

Personal prayer #6—*God, please give me wisdom.* This pinpoint prayer comes right from the lips of King Solomon, one of the world's wisest men. When told that God would grant him anything he asked for, Solomon had the sense to pray for wisdom instead of personal gain or riches (see 1 Kings 3:9). God gave Solomon wisdom and discernment that helped him lead Israel into an unmatched time of peace and national prosperity. God blessed Solomon's desire for wisdom.

How many decisions have you made in the past year that you wish you could change? What relational choices, personal investments, moral lapses, or career moves haunt you today because you didn't seek God's wisdom and discernment? James 1:5 exhorts every Christ-follower who lacks wisdom (that's pretty much all of us) to seek it from God. James promises that God will download his wisdom and insight into the minds of those who are humble enough to ask for it.

Are you willing to seek God's wisdom? What course are you on right now that needs to be reconsidered? You

It's Okay to Ask

face hundreds, if not thousands, of decisions—large and small—on a daily basis. Each has the potential to bring blessing or chaos into your life. More importantly, each can have profound spiritual effects on God's kingdom. Why risk the negative results in your life that stem from bad choices? Pray for God's wisdom.

Holy God, I humbly ask that you make me wise. Please give me your wisdom, insight, and discernment. Help me choose well in the daily aspects of my life. Help me honor you in the decisions I make every day. Please give me your wisdom.

Personal prayer #7—*God, please make me a "so be it" Christian.* One of my biblical heroes is the innocent and almost childlike figure of Mary. Although chosen to be the mother of our Savior, she couldn't have been more than thirteen or fourteen when she was called by God to her imposing task. Yet Mary showed a profound level of obedience and commitment to God's will. In his Gospel, Luke gave us the account of the angel Gabriel's announcement of God's history-making plans for Mary. Her response, especially for someone so young, astounds me: "I am the Lord's servant. . . . May it be to me as you have said" (Luke 1:38). I love the radical nature of Mary's answer. She didn't negotiate, she didn't complain, and she didn't whine. Mary simply acknowledged her position as the Lord's slave and then uttered one of the purest and simplest expressions of radical obedience in the Bible: "May it be to me as you have said." In other words, "So be it."

Are you a "so be it" Christian? Do you have the same attitude of no-holds-barred obedience modeled by this first-century Jewish teenager? Have you crossed the line of radical submission to God's will? If not, then start praying this pinpoint prayer for your life: *Lord, make me a "so be it" Christian.* That simple pinpoint prayer radically changed my life.

Years ago I came to a critical crossroads in my life. I was up to my ears in unforgiveness, abiding anger, relational inauthenticity, and spiritual disorder. I was a mess. I knew that I needed to face the music and begin the healing process, but I was afraid of what it would cost me. My inner black cauldron of emotional pain would have to be opened. Years of relational and family dysfunction would have to be confronted. My own sin and pitiful coping mechanisms would have to be brought into the light. In short, if I wanted to get healthy, I could expect a lot of pain.

Now, I like to think that I'm as tough as the next guy, maybe tougher. But when faced with the choice of deliberately walking into a season of emotional chaos, my survival instincts tend to kick in. Why hurt myself in the name of being healthy when I can continue in my unhealthiness and avoid the chaos that authenticity brings? But try as I might to avoid the Spirit's not-so-subtle promptings, I knew I needed to face my dark side.

I remember the very day I went for a long walk on a country road not far from my home. I wrestled with God and weighed the pros and cons and potential costs of bringing all my baggage into the light. There was no easy out; if I got honest, things were going to get rough. But if I didn't, I could pretty much count on having an emotional breakdown in the not-so-distant future.

Somewhere on that country road, I reached a critical watershed in my life. I crossed what I now call my "so be it" line. I decided that I needed to get healthy, face my pain, and do whatever it took to become the man God was requiring me to be. I readily accepted the implications and relational chaos that I knew would come. I remember saying out loud, "So be it." And at that moment, I was free.

My life changed instantly. The pain and relational chaos did come. I had to have some brutal conversations with family members. I had to forgive and seek forgiveness. I spent countless hours in a counselor's office sorting through all my emotional baggage. But it was worth every moment of it. As an adult Christian, my "so be it" moment was the most important of my life. Since then, I have prayed nearly every day for God to continue to give me a "so be it" mind-set. I will not negotiate with God. I refuse to arm wrestle or posture with my Creator. I am the Lord's slave; may it be to me as he has said.

Are you a "so be it" Christian? Have you crossed the line of radical obedience? Pray for a "so be it" mind-set. Tell God that you left your rights at the altar when you gave your life to Jesus. Tell him you will not negotiate, you will not posture, and you will not bargain. Close the door of obedience behind you. When you do, know that the best years of your Christian life lie ahead of you. Become a "so be it" Christian.

O God, make me radically obedient. Give me a heart like Mary's. I am your servant; may it be to me as you desire.

Don't Forget Your Parachute

There are countless other pinpoint prayers you can pray for yourself. Get into the habit of writing your initials next to Bible verses that state what you want God to do in you. The Bible is your best source for pinpoint prayers that God answers. Don't be shy about asking him to favor, protect, and guide you. Don't dare jump out into hostile spiritual territory until you've fully covered your heart, your relationships, your career, and your faith with powerful pinpoint praying.

Discussion Questions

1. Think about the tragic opening story of the parachute instructor. How prepared are you each day when you jump out into the world?
2. In your times of prayer, how much of it do you spend praying for yourself? What do you pray for?
3. The author argued that since he is the person who can most damage his ministry and relationships, he should pray most for himself. How do you feel about that philosophy?
4. Do you have any biblical promises that you are praying for yourself? If so, what are they? If not, what would it take for you to find some?
5. Have you ever had the kind of "so be it" moment that the author described? What happened?
6. In light of this chapter, how will you pray for yourself differently?

It's Okay to Ask

10

UGH!

Pinpoint Praying
When You Don't Know How to Pray

*In the same way, the Spirit helps us in our weakness.
We do not know what we ought to pray for.*

Romans 8:26

I met Carie when she was just nineteen. My first memory of her is from a baptism party for our church on Lake Austin. I was driving a boat, offering people wild and fun inner-tube rides. When I asked who wanted to go first, the cute little nineteen-year-old bounded out of the boat and onto the tube. I had never seen her before, but she was full of life and zeal and youthful energy.

Over the next decade, Carie became a vital part of our church and a close personal friend. She volunteered in our music and drama ministries, served on our church staff, and served as my personal assistant. In many ways, she was like a little sister to me. I watched Carie walk through a painful divorce, return to school to complete her college degree, navigate the unexpected death of her father, and deal with her own increasing struggles with rheumatoid arthritis. I talked with Carie at length about her hopes and dreams: Would she ever remarry? Would she ever have a professional acting career? Would she feel weak and arthritic for the rest of her life? What did God have for her? In all her questionings and struggles, Carie never doubted God or became angry with him. She had a faith that simply wouldn't budge. She was one of the most joy-filled and dependent Christ-followers I've ever known.

On a Monday in late November 2005, just a few months before her thirty-third birthday, doctors told Carie that she had an ovarian cyst that needed to be removed. They scheduled her for a relatively routine procedure a few days later. Even though Carie didn't feel well, she continued to come to work at church. That Wednesday we prayed in a team meeting and asked God to help her feel better. On Thursday, after enduring a series of blood tests, Carie chose to work the rest of the day, still in the surgical scrubs she had worn to the hospital that morning. On Friday Carie went in for her one-day surgery—a routine laparoscopy. On Sunday she died.

The doctors still aren't sure what happened. The cyst was actually on her intestine, not her ovary, and she had complications from the intestinal surgery. Doctors also discovered a massive, benign tumor inside Carie's heart chamber that greatly inhibited her blood flow and limited her intestine's ability to heal. Two days of additional operations and desperate measures to save Carie's life followed, but her heart finally succumbed to the relentless pressure it was under. I was standing near the foot of Carie's bed, along with an elder from our church and another member of our staff, while the crash team worked feverishly to resuscitate Carie. It was a nightmarish scene.

Carie was pronounced dead at 10:21 on Sunday night. In three horrific days, I had lost a very close friend, a co-worker, and someone for whom I felt very responsible. We buried Carie the following Wednesday, the day before Thanksgiving. And then I stopped praying.

It wasn't so much that I stopped praying deliberately; it was more like I just couldn't pray. I had shifted into ministry overdrive during the three-day vigil at the hospital. There were dozens of Carie's friends, small group members, and family who needed care, all of whom were as shocked and hurting over Carie's unbelievably bad turn of events as I was. They needed ministering to. I forced myself into a sort of spiritual adrenaline rush that didn't go away until after Carie's funeral. It wasn't until days later that I realized I couldn't pray. I felt as if I had been punched in the stomach, spiritually speaking. And much like someone with no air in his lungs, I couldn't even draw a breath to talk to God. I wanted and needed to pray, but I couldn't. My prayer mechanism was broken. I was a man with a wounded soul who desperately needed to talk with God but couldn't. And there wasn't a thing I could do about it.

Have you been there? I imagine so. There's nothing particularly unique about the loss I suffered or my spirit's response to it. If you've lived through your own life crises, then you may have experienced the same thing.

Dealing with Spiritual Blackouts

I'm writing this chapter in the month of April, but the weather in Austin feels like it's late August. Temperatures have been soaring into the low hundreds, and because of all the sudden air conditioner use, the local utility company has been caught unprepared. Recently on an exceptionally hot day and in an effort to avoid a complete statewide electrical failure, local utility officials staged rolling blackouts by shutting off power in various parts of the city at random times. Without warning, traffic lights stopped functioning, computers shut down, elevators stopped running, and entire sections of the city went dark. The demand

When you suffer spiritual blackout, you are not sinning.

for power exceeded the utility's ability to supply it. The result in Austin was several hours of traffic congestion, inconvenience, and even some political fallout.

When Carie died, I experienced a spiritual rolling blackout. My ability to function spiritually basically came to a grinding halt. The circumstances, stress, and pain of the moment overpowered me. I wasn't living in sin or out of fellowship with God. I wasn't being punished or abandoned by God. He was right there with me, but I just couldn't talk to him. I didn't have the energy to pray.

Spiritual blackouts happen when life throws more information at you than you can process spiritually. Remember Job? He learned in just a matter of minutes that he'd lost all of his herds and flocks, most of his servants, and all of his children. What's the rest of the book of Job about? Spiritual blackout. Job was hurting, and he needed time to process the pain and confusion he was feeling. He needed help talking to God; he simply couldn't do it on his own.

You need to know that when you suffer spiritual blackout, you are not sinning. God is not punishing you, and he has not abandoned you. Prayerlessness—your lack of discipline in or commitment to prayer—is not the same as being unable to pray. The former is caused by sin, the latter by suffering. Spiritual blackout is not a condition from which you need to repent. You can't. Don't let some well-meaning brother or sister tell you that you're sinning if your soul is in spiritual blackout. You didn't choose to stop praying. You simply can't.

Be patient in the crisis. The air will find its way back into your lungs. You will be able to pray again. But in the meantime, it's good to know that you're not alone. There is a helper even in the midst of spiritual blackout.

The Holy Spirit to the Rescue

To those of us who have ever lost our ability to pray, the Bible offers an amazing promise in Romans 8:26–27. To me, this is one of the sweetest and most encouraging promises in the Bible regarding pinpoint prayer. Paul writes,

> And the Holy Spirit helps us in our distress. For we don't even know what we should pray for, nor how we should pray. But the Holy Spirit prays for us with groanings that cannot be expressed in words. And the Father who knows all hearts knows what the Spirit is saying, for the Spirit pleads for us believers in harmony with God's own will.
>
> NLT

Ugh!

The believers Paul addresses here lived in Rome, one of the most spiritually hostile cities in the world. At any moment, they could have been arrested, had their property confiscated, had family members taken from them, been tortured, or even been killed simply because they were Christians. They certainly endured seasons where their grief was so intense and their circumstances so severe that their spiritual systems simply shut down. To those hurting believers, Paul offers these marvelous words.

He offers them to us as well. If you're struggling with your prayers, this is a critical verse for you to know and understand. Let's think about what it tells us.

Spiritual blackouts are normal. They're not good, but neither are they a deathblow to your relationship with God. Paul told Timothy that all who try to live godly lives will be persecuted (see 2 Tim. 3:12); he could have also said that all who try to be people of prayer will suffer blackouts. Unfortunately, rolling spiritual blackouts are normal.

The fact that the Bible addresses spiritual blackouts tells us that they're common and that God wants to comfort us in them. In Romans 8, Paul acknowledges that there are times when we don't know how to pray. He doesn't seem panicked by this truth. Instead, he draws comfort from the Holy Spirit's ability to do for him what he could not do for himself.

Are you in spiritual blackout? Have you temporarily lost your ability to pray? Don't panic. Don't let Satan tell you that you lack faith or that you've failed as a Christian. What you're experiencing is normal. **The Holy Spirit is our hope in times of blackout.** In this sweeping promise, Paul tells us of three roles the Holy Spirit plays when we're in blackout. First, he helps us. The word picture Paul paints is that of a joint effort or cooperation. If you're digging a hole, a helper is someone who picks up a shovel and assists you in the task. That's what the Holy Spirit does in crisis. When you're in the deep pit of spiritual distress, the Holy Spirit is your promised helper. He jumps into the mire with you and leads you through the trial. He helps you in your weakness. When Carie died, I was too weak—too spiritually winded—to pray, and that's typically the case in any spiritual blackout. That's when the Holy Spirit does his best work. He thrives in our weakness.

Second, Paul tells us that the Holy Spirit prays for us. Actually, *prays* isn't a strong enough word. Paul's word is *intercedes*. That's a more accurate picture—the Holy Spirit pleads, wrestles, and rallies God vigorously on our behalf. When life's crises have left you dead in the water spiritually, rest in knowing that the Holy Spirit is praying for you.

Think about that for a minute. He prays *for you*. That means he prays in place of you, instead of you. When you can't pray, the Holy Spirit assumes the role of your spiritual stand-in. He prays to God the prayers that you would pray if you were able. But he also prays about you, concerning you, and regarding you. In other words, when you're in spiritual blackout, the Holy Spirit becomes your primary advocate before God.

Third, not only does the Holy Spirit pray for us, but he does so according to God's will. When the Holy Spirit steps in for you in times of blackout, he not only knows your heart but he also knows God's. He knows just what you need and just what God wants. When he prays for you, he doesn't pray simply what you would pray if you could. He prays exactly what God's will is for you. It's like having your own personal lobbyist in heaven, one who is without sin and has perfect motives. Your holy lobbyist speaks to God, pleads with God, and appeals to God on your behalf, and he does so in such a way that God's answer is always yes!

As you can see, spiritual blackout can actually be a time of great blessing to Christ-followers. Even though you're in pain and your world seems to be crumbling in around you, even though you're so spiritually wounded that you can't pray, your prayers are still being heard. Your holy advocate never ceases pleading with God for you. He builds the perfect case before the Father for your blessing, your protection, your healing, and your provision. As a result, when the fog finally lifts and the blackout ends, you can look back and know that God was with you. The greatest pinpoint pray-er in all of heaven is interceding for you in exact alignment with the will of God. Because of that, he can turn your season of crisis into a season of favor, blessing, and growth.

This astounding promise in Romans 8 tells us one more thing about prayer in spiritual blackout: it's impossible for you to pray wrong. Let me illustrate what I mean.

Ugh!

We have a delightful young woman on our church staff whom we've nicknamed "the translator." She has an uncanny ability to understand what each of us is saying and restate it in a way in which the others can get it as well. Sometimes when things get tense in a discussion and we're having trouble hearing each other's points, we'll instinctively turn to "the translator" for interpretation. She'll smile and say, "Here's what they're trying to say." Then she'll give a clear, concise, and convincing restatement of the respective point of view. The results are amazing. Typically, emotions settle down and compromise is quickly reached. All decision-making bodies should have such a gifted person.

Now imagine you're in spiritual blackout. You can't pray. All you can muster is an occasional moan or a brief "God, help me" kind of prayer. But that's all your translator, the Holy Spirit, needs. We've already seen that the Spirit interprets our prayers and restates them to God in accordance with his will. That means that in times of blackout, it is impossible for you to pray wrong! Regardless of how desperate, how wounded, or how gritty your prayers are, you can't miss God when you're stumbling through spiritual blackout. The holy translator promises to catch your mangled prayer and deliver it to God in a presentable fashion. It's like being guaranteed you'll make a basket every time you shoot the ball, regardless of how poorly you may be shooting. Just give it your best shot and throw it up there, and let the Holy Spirit take it from there.

I find this to be an incredibly comforting promise when I'm struggling in prayer. Sometimes it can be really difficult to discern God's will. Sometimes it's difficult to see God's plan and purpose. That's why

> The greatest pinpoint pray-er in all of heaven is interceding for you in exact alignment with the will of God.

he gave us these verses. The Holy Spirit promises to hear our barely audible prayer gasps and to restate them to God for us. He promises not only to represent our best interests but also to represent God's. Can you think of a more powerful or encouraging prayer promise, especially if you're in a season of blackout? It takes all the risk out of praying. You're not going to offend God or miss God or blow it before God in your weakened condition. God knows that seasons of blackout are going to come, and he has sent his Holy Spirit to make sure that we can pray well, even when we can't pray at all.

You probably know the verse that follows Romans 8:26–27, but maybe you haven't made the connection between the two. Romans 8:28 says, "And we know that God causes everything to work together for the good of those who love God and are called according to his purpose" (NLT). You've heard that verse, and you know that God works out everything for good in a believer's life. Perhaps what you didn't know was that he does so in the midst of spiritual blackout through the ongoing prayers of the Holy Spirit.

Are you in blackout? Don't fret. You can't pray? Don't panic. God is pulling you through this. Good will come from this. You're being prayed for by the most discerning and powerful force in the universe. His prayer for you is reaching the heart of God. And in this case, you really couldn't have said it better yourself.

Survival Tips for Spiritual Blackout

Since it is inevitable that we're going to endure seasons of spiritual blackout, and since the Spirit has promised to pray for us when we can't pray for ourselves, what's our responsibility? What can we do to help us remain faithful to God and to ensure that we come through the storm with our faith intact? Here are some suggestions.

Keep reading the Bible. You may not be able to talk to God, but you can certainly let him talk to you. It's critical that in times of spiritual blackout, you continue to lean into God through his Word. Blackout is no time for a spiritual hunger strike. You can't afford to be completely cut off from God, so keep reading the Bible.

When I was in my blackout, I read the Bible for extended periods of time every day. I desperately needed to connect with God, and the Bible was the only way I seemed to be able to do so. The Scriptures kept me anchored to God in a time when I could have easily drifted away. If you're in blackout, it's imperative that you understand that truth. You can survive not praying for a while, based on the Holy Spirit's generous intercession for you. You can't survive an extended period of neither praying nor reading. You'll simply dry up spiritually. Don't add spiritual famine to your spiritual blackout. Stay in the Bible.

Stay in community. Spiritual blackout is no time to fly solo. We don't function well in isolation even when we *can* pray, so it should be obvious that we need other Christians even more when we can't. When you suffer blackout, don't withdraw from God's church. You need the community, comfort, and prayers of God's people.

Because I'm a pastor, I couldn't withdraw when Carie died. My job required that I stay surrounded by godly brothers and sisters. But we can be in a crowd of Christians and still be isolated. We can be inauthentic and act like everything is fine. We all know the pressure that church cultures can produce for us to appear strong and mature. Who wants to admit to another Christian that they can't pray?

Actually, I did. I was very deliberate about being authentic during the days of my spiritual

> It's critical that in times of spiritual blackout, you continue to lean into God through his Word.

darkness. I felt no need to fake it before God's people. I knew that God was sovereign and that he had allowed Carie to die. I also knew that my inability to pray wasn't due to any sin or lack of maturity on my part. I was in a dark season of spiritual blackout, and I saw no reason to hide that from the church.

I remember one specific service where I confessed to the church that I couldn't pray. I was very honest. I told them that since Carie's death, something had been broken inside me. I told them that I wanted to pray and needed to pray, but I just couldn't. I told them how much I needed God's help and theirs.

The church's response was overwhelming. Immediately after the service and in the days that followed, I was swamped with encouraging words, hugs, and prayers. God comforted me, strengthened me, and loved on me through the wonderfully tangible outlet of his people. I had chosen to be authentic and to lean into community, and God blessed me for it.

Are you in blackout? Don't hide from the church. Don't push away those who want to care for you. You need them more than you know. Your inability to pray is nothing for which you need to be ashamed. Be real and authentic about your spiritual condition. You'll find that God will minister to you and restore your wounded soul through the loving and genuine care of his church.

Affirm the goodness of God. When in blackout, it's easy to see God as an adversary. That's the lie that Satan loves to tell: God has become your enemy. His slanderous accusations of God might sound something like this: *Hey, loser! Where's your God now? If you're so spiritual, why can't you pray? And if God is so great and loves you so much, why isn't he helping you? God has obviously given up on you, so you might as well throw in the towel too.*

In the face of such withering spiritual oppression, it's important that we remind ourselves of what we know to be true about God. Jesus told us that truth sets us free (see John 8:32), and we know that truth is the best weapon against Satan's lies. Stop and affirm that God is good. Focus on promises like Romans 8:28 that tell you God is doing good even when you can't initially see it. Be still before God and remind yourself that he is God (see Ps. 46:10). Remember that even though you can't pray, you are being prayed for by the Holy Spirit.

Spiritual blackout doesn't have to be devastating to your relationship with or faith in God. Don't let the enemy mislead you. Fill your heart and mind with what you know about God. Rest in his goodness and trust that he is strong in your current weakness.

Worship. In Psalm 22, David confessed that he was in a season of spiritual blackout. Listen to his honest struggle with God: "My God, my God, why have You forsaken me? Far from my deliverance are the words of my groaning. O my God, I cry by day, but You do not answer; and by night, but I have no rest" (vv. 1–2 NASB). David acknowledged that all he could do was groan before God, and even that was ineffective. He felt no connection to his heavenly Father. But then he continued, "Yet You are holy, O You who are enthroned upon the praises of Israel" (v. 3 NASB). The first four words in that verse may be the most important words in the Bible to a believer in blackout—"Yet You are holy." In that simple phrase of confession, David reminded himself that God was still sovereign and was still in control of his circumstances. His moment of worship gave him the eternal perspective he desperately needed.

Worship does that. It reminds us of God's holy nature and his absolute control. It helps us see things from God's point of view. Along with the discipline of Bible reading, Christians in blackout need to immerse themselves in worship settings. Their praise of God will usher them into his holy presence and grant them the hope and perspective they need.

In the early 1990s, my favorite worship album was called *Lion of Judah*, and the music was led by a relatively unknown worship leader from San Antonio named Dave Bell. His music was some of the most inspiring and stirring that I have ever heard. Dave's lyrics spoke to me and led me into God's presence in a unique and powerful way. For over two years, I used the cassette tape of *Lion of Judah* as a worship prompter in my own heart.

Gradually I stopped listening to the tape as much. I eventually lost track of it altogether. It had been in my office but was lost in our church's multiple moves and office settings over the years. I tried to buy another copy on several occasions, but the music was out of print, and no copies were available on the Internet. I gave up trying to find it. But I did miss it. I found that in very special or critical seasons of my life I really longed for some good Dave Bell–led worship. Carie's death was one of those times.

Two days after Carie died, I was standing in the office of our church's director of creative arts, discussing Carie's funeral plans. As I turned to leave, my eyes caught a cassette on the bookshelf. It was *Lion of Judah*. I had been in that office and looked at that bookshelf countless times before and had never seen that tape, but on that day, there it was. It was a gift from God.

I devoured that tape. I kept it playing in my car whenever I was driving. Those old songs helped me express my love for God and my confidence in him at a time when my heart was overwhelmed with pain. The moments of worship I had alone with Christ in my car sustained me through those difficult days and prepared me for what lay ahead—Carie's funeral. I honestly didn't know how I could lead it. I couldn't pray, and I certainly couldn't preach. How could I possibly lead others through their efforts to grieve for Carie? The answer came through the Holy Spirit's pinpoint prayers for me and through the eternal perspective I gained in worship.

The night before Carie's funeral, I had to teach at our church's midweek worship service. As I was leading the church in prayer (or, rather, trying to), I had a vision. It wasn't a vision like the book of Revelation or Joseph's dreams were visions; it was more like a mental picture. I saw a massive throng of people, much like a huge crowd at a football game, standing in joy-filled worship before God's throne. I was aware that there were many people in the crowd, but the only face I could see completely was Carie's. She was there before God in completely undistracted and joyful worship of God.

While I was seeing that picture, I was up on our stage praying before the church. Actually, I know the Holy Spirit was praying through me and for me, because what I said at that point in the prayer was something I'd never said or thought before. I prayed, "Lord, we're minus a worshiper tonight," and then the tears came. I just broke down sobbing. I couldn't even finish the prayer. I sat down and cried during most of the worship segment, my pain just spilling out of me.

No doubt I was crying out of grief and sadness, but I was also crying out of the sheer profundity of what I'd seen. Our church had lost a worshiper, but heaven had gained one. For some reason, the weight of that reality blew me away. Seeing Carie in that crowd humbled me and gave me a completely different perspective. I am convinced that what prepared me for those brief moments of insight was my own private worship of the Lord with the help of an old, worn-out worship tape. God softened the soil of my heart and prepared me for what he wanted to show me. He used worship as a means of communication with me when I couldn't pray, and that's what saved me. God met me in worship. "Yet You are holy."

The next day, I was able to lead Carie's funeral with strength, confidence, and even a little joy. It was still difficult, but the edge had been taken off. My simple acts of pinpoint worship when I couldn't offer pinpoint prayers had set my captive soul free.

Are you in blackout? Dive into worship. God will meet you there, love you there, and heal you there. Praise attracts the presence of God, and when you're in spiritual blackout, that's what you need most—God's holy presence.

Discussion Questions

1. Have you ever experienced the kind of spiritual blackout that the author described? What happened? How did you feel?
2. How often do you feel that you don't know how to pray? How do you feel now, knowing that the Holy Spirit prays for you even when you can't?
3. The author spoke of the importance of Bible reading, community, affirming God's goodness, and worship in times of blackout. What role do these important spiritual disciplines play in your life?
4. What spiritual dilemma are you facing? What would you say to the Holy Spirit, knowing that he is praying for you? What would you ask him to say to God on your behalf?
5. In light of this chapter, how will you pray differently?

Ugh!

Conclusion

I believe in prayer.
 I opened this book with that sentence, and I need to return to it now. I believe in prayer. You do too. I know that because otherwise you wouldn't have read this far. You are now more equipped to be a pinpoint pray-er. You can see with better vision the unlimited world of impact and answers that awaits those willing to pray.
 Enough said. It's time to pray. May God show himself mighty on your behalf and on behalf of those for whom you offer pinpoint prayers. Let's get to it.

APPENDIX

100 Pinpoint Prayers from the Psalms

Below are one hundred pinpoint prayers from the Psalms. Included are examples of prayers for your children, your spouse, your church, yourself, and your unbelieving friends. These are just a sampling of countless pinpoint prayers waiting to be discovered in the pages of Scripture.

1. *Father, help my children delight in your law and meditate on your word day and night.* Psalm 1:2

2. *Dear God, let this ministry be "like a tree planted by streams of water, which yields its fruit in season and whose leaf does not wither." Cause all that we do to prosper.* Psalm 1:3

3. *O Lord, make this city your inheritance and the ends of the earth your possession.* Psalm 2:8

4. *Father, teach Tom to serve you with fear and to rejoice with trembling.* Psalm 2:11

5. *Mighty God, be a shield about me. Shine your glory on me and be the lifter of my head.* Psalm 3:3

6. *Lord, help my wife not to fear ten thousand enemies opposing her, because she trusts in you.* Psalm 3:6

7. *"Answer me when I call to you, O my righteous God. Give me relief from my distress; be merciful to me and hear my prayer."* Psalm 4:1

8. *Lord, I ask that you make my children godly and set them apart for yourself.* Psalm 4:3

9. *Father, please fill my wife with greater joy than what any material thing can provide.* Psalm 4:7

10. *Holy God, cause my children to lie down and sleep in peace. Help them dwell in safety.* Psalm 4:8

11. *Father, in the morning "you hear my voice; in the morning I lay my requests before you and wait in expectation." Thank you for answering me.* Psalm 5:3

12. *Dear God, help my children to "take refuge in you and be glad; let them ever sing for joy. Spread your protection over them" that they may love your name and rejoice in you.* Psalm 5:11

13. *Father, I pray you will hear Steve's cry for mercy and accept his prayer.* Psalm 6:9

14. *O righteous God who searches minds and hearts, I pray for this city. "Bring to an end the violence of the wicked and make the righteous secure."* Psalm 7:9

15. *Lord, you are righteous and you love justice; I pray that my wife will be holy and will see your face.* Psalm 11:7

16. *Merciful God, in my city "the wicked freely strut about when what is vile is honored among men." Please humble us and bring revival to this city.* Psalm 12:8

17. *Lord, let my children trust in your unfailing love and rejoice in your salvation.* Psalm 13:5

18. *Holy God, I will sing to you, for you have been good to me.* Psalm 13:6

19. *Please keep my family safe, O God, for in you we take refuge.* Psalm 16:1

20. *Father, humble me. "Though you probe my heart and examine me at night, though you test me, you will find nothing; I have resolved that my mouth will not sin."* Psalm 17:3

21. *Mighty God, please keep my children as the apple of your eye; hide them in the shadow of your wings.* Psalm 17:8

22. *Jesus, you are my rock, my fortress, and my deliverer, the one in whom I take refuge. You are my shield and the horn of my salvation, my stronghold.* Psalm 18:2

23. *Lord, I pray for my wife. Make her feet like the feet of a deer; enable her to stand on the heights.* Psalm 18:33

24. *For my son, I pray that you will train his hands for war. Teach him to fight with your spiritual weapons.* Psalm 18:34

25. *For my daughters, I pray that you will broaden the path beneath them so that their ankles do not turn.* Psalm 18:36

26. *Father, as the people in this ministry seek your face, give us the desires of our hearts and make all our plans succeed.* Psalm 20:4

27. *Mighty God, you are my shepherd; I shall not be in want.* Psalm 23:1

28. *Lord, I pray you will restore Tim's soul.* Psalm 23:3

Appendix

29. *Holy God, please give my children clean hands and pure hearts. Keep them from pursuing idols or from swearing by anything false.* Psalm 24:4

30. *"Show me your ways, O LORD, teach me your paths; guide me in your truth and teach me, for you are God my Savior, and my hope is in you all day long."* Psalm 25:4–5

31. *"For the sake of your name, O LORD, forgive my iniquity, though it is great."* Psalm 25:11

32. *Father, I pray for my kids. Let integrity and uprightness protect them, because their hope is in you.* Psalm 25:21

33. *"My heart says of you, 'Seek his face!' Your face, LORD, I will seek."* Psalm 27:8

34. *Lord, I pray for my wife. Help her to be strong, to take heart, and to wait for you.* Psalm 27:14

35. *Father, I pray for Jessica. Please turn her wailing into dancing; remove her sackcloth and clothe her with joy, that her heart may sing to you and not be silent. O Lord, may she give you thanks forever.* Psalm 30:11–12

36. *Lord, be my wife's hiding place. Please protect her from trouble and surround her with songs of deliverance.* Psalm 32:7

37. *Father, please instruct my children and teach them the way they should go. Counsel them and watch over them.* Psalm 32:8

38. *"May your unfailing love rest upon us, O LORD, even as we put our hope in you."* Psalm 33:22

39. *Father, I pray for my children. Let your angels encamp around them and deliver them.* Psalm 34:7

40. *Jesus, please help Larry to taste and see that you are good.* Psalm 34:8

41. *Father, contend with those who contend with this ministry; fight against those who fight us.* Psalm 35:1

42. *Holy Lord, as I delight myself in you, please give me the desires of my heart.* Psalm 37:4

43. *Dear God, "send forth your light and your truth, let them guide me; let them bring me to your holy mountain, to the place where you dwell."* Psalm 43:3

44. *Mighty Lord, be my family's refuge and strength, our ever-present help in trouble.* Psalm 46:1

45. *Father, help Sally to be still and know that you are God.* Psalm 46:10

46. *"Have mercy on me, O God, according to your unfailing love; according to your great compassion blot out my transgressions. Wash away all my iniquity and cleanse me from my sin."* Psalm 51:1–2

47. *O God, create in Jim a pure heart, and renew a steadfast spirit within him.* Psalm 51:10

48. *Father, help my wife to cast her cares upon you. Please sustain her and never let her fall.* Psalm 55:22

49. *Lord, when my children are afraid, teach them to trust in you.* Psalm 56:3

50. *Holy Savior, help Bill to find rest in you alone. Let him discover that salvation comes only from you.* Psalm 62:1

51. *Mighty Lord, let my children trust in you at all times. Teach them to pour out their hearts to you in prayer.* Psalm 62:8

52. *Father, as we pray to you, "answer us with awesome deeds of righteousness."* Psalm 65:5

53. *Holy God, please be gracious to my children and bless them; cause your sweet face to shine upon them.* Psalm 67:1

Appendix

54. *Father, I pray for this city. Summon your power;* "show us your strength, O God, as you have done before." Psalm 68:28

55. *Lord, please protect my integrity.* "May those who hope in you not be disgraced because of me." *May those who seek you not be put to shame because of anything I do or say.* Psalm 69:6

56. *Jesus, let Benji see you and be glad; let his heart seek you and live.* Psalm 69:32

57. *Father, please always be with my children; hold them each by their right hand. Guide them through life with your great counsel, and afterward take them to your glory.* Psalm 73:23–24

58. *Father, I pray for this nation.* "Restore us again, O God our Savior, and put away your displeasure toward us." Psalm 85:4

59. *Lord,* "revive us again, that your people may rejoice in you." Psalm 85:6

60. *Jesus, please show Charlie your unfailing love and grant him your salvation.* Psalm 85:7

61. "Teach me your way, O Lord, and I will walk in your truth; give me an undivided heart, that I may fear your name." Psalm 86:11

62. *Lord, I pray that John will call out to you as his God, his Father, his Rock, his salvation, and his deliverer.* Psalm 89:26

63. *Father, may your favor rest upon us. Please establish the work of our hands.* Psalm 90:17

64. *Lord, let my kids not fear* "the terror of night, nor the arrow that flies by day, nor the pestilence that stalks in the darkness, nor the plague that destroys at midday," *for you are with them.* Psalm 91:5–6

65. *Father, command your angels concerning my children, to guard them in all their ways.* Psalm 91:11

66. *Savior, please make known your salvation to Thomas; reveal your righteousness to him.* Psalm 98:2

67. *Father, help me to walk in my house with a blameless heart. I will set no vile thing before my eyes.* Psalm 101:2–3

68. *Lord, redeem this city for your name's sake; make your power known.* Psalm 106:8

69. *Savior, please send forth your word and heal Denny; rescue him from his grave.* Psalm 107:20

70. *Father, please give my wife peace and guide her to her desired haven.* Psalm 107:30

71. *Lord, make me a man of prayer.* Psalm 109:4

72. *Holy God, show your power in this city. "Let them know that it is your hand, that you, O LORD, have done it."* Psalm 109:27

73. *Father, help my children discover wisdom through fearing and revering you.* Psalm 111:10

74. *Lord, please make my children mighty in the land and bless them with your righteousness.* Psalm 112:2

75. *Mighty God, teach my children to be generous, to lend freely, and to conduct their affairs with justice.* Psalm 112:5

76. *Father, deliver Henry's soul from death, his eyes from tears, and his feet from stumbling. Cause him to walk before you in the land of the living.* Psalm 116:8–9

77. *Savior, please free Mike from his chains.* Psalm 116:16

78. *Lord, please make my way blameless; help me walk according to your law.* Psalm 119:1

79. *Father, help me to keep your law; I want to seek you with all my heart.* Psalm 119:2

Appendix

80. *O Lord, as I live according to your Word, help me keep my way pure.* Psalm 119:9

81. *Lord, help my son to hide your Word in his heart so that he won't sin against you.* Psalm 119:11

82. *Make me disciplined, O God, that I might meditate on your truths and consider your ways.* Psalm 119:15

83. *Precious Father, open the eyes of my children and help them to see wonderful truths in your Word.* Psalm 119:18

84. *Gentle Savior, when my kids stray from your commands, please rebuke them.* Psalm 119:21

85. *Lord, I pray for my wife. Let your law be her delight and your Spirit her counselor.* Psalm 119:24

86. *Holy God, please keep me from lying to myself; rather, let me live in the grace and truth of your Word.* Psalm 119:29

87. *Father, I pray for wisdom; help me "keep your law and obey it with all my heart."* Psalm 119:34

88. *Jesus, please turn my heart toward your Word and away from selfish gain.* Psalm 119:36

89. *Holy God, please create in my children a deep longing for your Word.* Psalm 119:40

90. *Holy God, please give me an audience before kings, that I may speak of your Word.* Psalm 119:46

91. *Holy Father, remember your promises to your servant, for they are my hope.* Psalm 119:49

92. *Lord, teach my children to hate wickedness and anything that opposes your holy law.* Psalm 119:53

93. *Dear God, I humbly ask that if I stray from your truth, you will afflict me so I will learn obedience to your Word.* Psalm 119:67

94. *Holy God, I pray that the words of your mouth will be "more precious to me than thousands of pieces of silver and gold."* Psalm 119:72

95. *Holy Father, help my wife not to focus on all the evil around her but rather to meditate on your teachings.* Psalm 119:95

96. *Dear God, help my children to love your law and meditate on it all day long.* Psalm 119:97

97. *Lord God, as my kids contemplate your Word, teach them to outthink and outreason your enemies.* Psalm 119:98

98. *Lord, let my wife find your words more pleasing than honey or any other earthly pleasure.* Psalm 119:103

99. *Mighty God, humble me before you. Teach me to reverence your name and to stand in awe of your laws.* Psalm 119:120

100. *Holy Father, I pray that you will move powerfully and quickly in our land, for your laws are being broken.* Psalm 119:126

Notes

1. Jim Collins and Jerry Porras, *Built to Last: Successful Habits of Visionary Companies* (New York: HarperCollins, 2002), 232–34.

2. Ron Kurtus, "Winston Churchill's 'Never Give In' Speech of 1941," *School for Champions*, November 25, 2005, www.school-for-champions.com/speeches/churchill_never_give_in.htm.

3. From the journal kept by Abby's mother, Wendy Jimmerson, for her daughter.

4. See www.Secretariat.com and www.Angelfire.com/jazz/nutbush.

5. "Man without Chute Films Own Death Plunge," *Associated Press*, April 6, 1988, www.aarrgghh.com/no_way/noChute.htm.

Will Davis Jr. is the founding and senior pastor of Austin Christian Fellowship in Austin, Texas. Will and his wife, Susie, have three children.

Visit www.**praybigbook**.com today!

You'll be inspired to:
- send a free "I Prayed for You Today" e-card to a friend
- watch the *Pray Big* video or listen to the audio sermon
- use free *Pray Big* sermon outlines and small group resources in your church

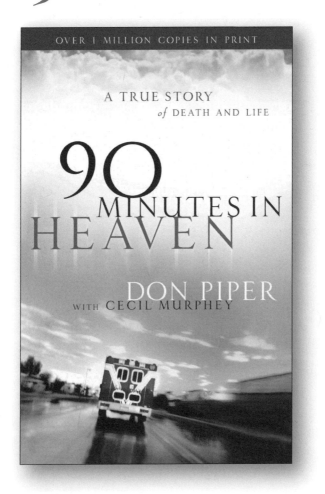